STORIES OF VIRTUE
IN BUSINESS

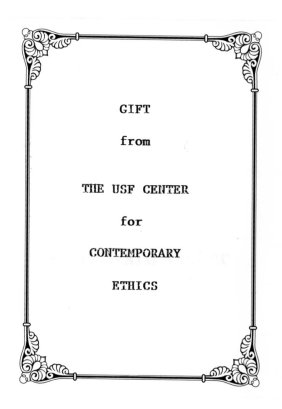

GIFT

from

THE USF CENTER

for

CONTEMPORARY

ETHICS

University Press of America, Inc.
Lanham • New York • London

Copyright © 1995 by
C. Edward Weber
University Press of America,® Inc.
4720 Boston Way
Lanham, Maryland 20706

3 Henrietta Street
London, WC2E 8LU England

Library of Congress Cataloging-in-Publication Data

Weber, C. Edward (Charles Edward).
Stories of virtue in business / C. Edward Weber.
p. cm.
1. Business ethics. 2. Social responsibility of business. 3. Virtue. I.
Title.
HF5387.W425   1995   174'.4--dc20   95-10749 CIP

ISBN 0-8191-9950-8 (pbk: alk: paper)

⊖™ The paper used in this publication meets the minimum
requirements of American National Standard for Information
Sciences—Permanence of Paper for Printed Library Materials,

TO SUZANNE

CONTENTS

INTRODUCTION

The book is a collection of stories about virtue in business. These stories were told to me when I asked business men and women to tell me about exemplary conduct that they had observed at work.[1] Questions are included after each story. Their purpose is to aid readers in interpreting the stories and giving them meaning. Also, the questions are intended to help readers apply the stories to their own situations.

Students, business and other observers have heard or read stories of managers' deceit and self-aggrandizement that reflect a culture of self-centeredness and greed. They see the great ethical failures that are detected and reported by the media and the legal system. However, these great failures are not events separate from ordinary conduct but flow from managers' frailty in many small decisions. Expediency, as a daily fare, fosters corruption in the business community.

Also we have heard stories about strong hearted decisions by business men and women -- actions that placed themselves and their organizations at risk and that achieved great good for the stakeholders. These decisions did not stand by themselves either, but flowed from the managers' integrity in many small decisions. Principled action on a routine basis closes the door to corruption.

My purpose is to collect stories about the little decisions that reflect the virtuous life. The stories are about the central

---

[1]I gratefully acknowledge the advice and suggestions of James J. Kratoska, Robert Manegold, Henry Mayer, David McLain, Gene Mucklin, Conrad Schaum, Rev. Richard Schlenker, Benson Soffer, Suzanne B. Weber, and Rev. Oliver F. Williams in conducting and interpreting my search; and I am grateful for the generosity, openness and trust of the many business men and women who told me their stories.

aspects of interpersonal relations within the business world. They illustrate honesty, truthfulness, respect, compassion and other virtues being lived by people in business. They touch on the fine borderline between professional proficiency and ethical conscience.

The stories are remarkable, but not astonishing. Many business people have faced similar situations and can identify with the storytellers and the people in the stories. Others, while experiencing similar situations as told in the stories, are skeptical about whether the actions are virtuous. Such actions can have "rough edges", and a virtuous life can also reflect human foibles.

In one, for example, the storyteller returns a friend's small gift because it may be against company policy. Some may see this as reflecting the storyteller's integrity -- adhering to his principles, while another may see a lack of compassion in his action. A second storyteller describes how his company was creating a climate of compassion, but the postscript portrays an action, destroying the new climate.

People's actions can be interpreted variously, and the interpretation can change with time. People can and do differ on whether concrete decisions were the best ethical choices. Stark ethical failures are easy to recognize, but it is more difficult to see the wisdom of decisions that balance ethical considerations. It is not always possible to know whether the action was virtuous at the time, but we sometimes need to reflect on it with hindsight. Stories may seem virtuous to some and less so to others. Hopefully, the meaning becomes clearer as the action unfolds and time passes.

My purpose is not an apologia for how ethics is practiced in business. I do not intend to minimize the great and small ethical failures that have occurred by focusing on exemplary conduct in the daily lives of business people. Neither am I seeking to redress observers' impressions of the extent of ethical failure. Rather, my aim is to describe principled conduct that has occurred in ordinary matters and on an ordinary basis.

My purpose is to give students, business people and other observers the opportunity to ponder these stories and reflect upon the role of virtue in their own professional lives.

Readers can agree or disagree with the storytellers' judgments on what conduct was ethical, and they can draw their own conclusions. The stories' protagonists are seeking the virtuous life, but not necessarily finding it; and readers may be in the same predicament. The stories are brief and the book can be picked up whenever the reader has a few moments. The book makes a good travel companion.

The readers can recreate their own stories by reflecting on the stories told here. Stories are a way for gaining an understanding of virtue so we can act virtuously. My hope is to add the book's stories to those being told about people in business.[1] Eventually these stories will lead to archetypal stories that guide ethical conduct.

Not all of the stories have 'good endings'; and some stories -- that end well -- have ambiguous beginnings. The passage for other stories takes place on slippery slopes. My impression from collecting these stories is that virtue is fragile. The stories' protagonists sometimes experience action that is less than virtuous -- inconsistent with their principles; and this leads to committing themselves to virtuous action. The ethical dilemma is part of the human condition. Its been with us and will continue to be with us, and our task is to consider it on a continuing basis.

Today's business professional is faced with a growing demand for ethical conduct. The demand is driven by society's reawakening from its moral slumber to the importance of principled action. The business environment is too complex to navigate without an ethical compass. The conflicting statutory and civil requirements provide an executive with little or no guidance as the competing objectives of the welfare state are played out in the business arena. It is a climate where the rules are inconsistent and changing, and society seems to profess moral neutrality and practice moral indifference. In fact,

---

[1] See James E. Liebig, *Business Ethics: Profiles in Civic Virtue* (Golden, Colorado: Fulcrum Publishing, 1990); Michael Rion, *The Responsible Manager* (New York: Harper & Row, 1989); and Barbara Ley Toffler, *Tough Choices: Managers Talk Ethics* (New York: John Wiley & Sons, 1986).

calling someone virtuous can be pejorative. In this climate, maxims of moral behavior provide the only foundation for integrity.

The book can be very useful as a basis for class discussion either in a course on business ethics or in continuing education for business executives. I have used the stories in programs for mid-level and senior managers. It can be used as an instrument in applying ethical principles already learned or as a means to help students and managers see the problems and their complexity. The fact that there are no clearly right or wrong answers makes them especially useful for probing ethical conduct. The stories bring ethical considerations into the open; and, so, can awaken readers' sense of decency and fair play that is the first step in living an integrated moral life.

The stories bring the business professional into intimate contact with moral dilemmas, deliberations and outcomes of those who have been in the process of formulating ethical maxims from their own experiences. These stories show the risks and costs, as well as the rewards of an ethical business life. The stories show the origins of the ethical problem that always is something small with the potential to grow more visible, consequential and unmanageable.

VIRTUE

Stories of virtue are uncommon, whether in business or in other contexts, for virtue demands discernment of the right course and the courage to act. Virtue is the long habit (disposition) of acting uprightly with insight into what is good. It connotes that the person *repeatedly* makes wise choices when faced with dilemmas that have conflicting alternatives, each with good and bad aspects. Virtuous acts go the middle way midst dilemmas, and this is found, in retrospect, to be the right way. A single choice, however, does not denote the virtuous person, but the habit of making such choices does.[1]

Virtuous acts flow from interpreting principles -- also described as virtues -- in situations being lived by business. The principles are rooted in human experience and only then are they embedded in theory. Principles that seem to fit the experience of business are:

Adhering to the law;
Avoiding harm to others;
Honesty;
Respect;
Justice (honoring the rights and duties of others and ourselves);
Promise keeping (commitment);
Courage;
Compassion.

Business needs to understand what action to take, to have the courage to take action in the midst of conflicting claims, to be compassionate with those harmed by the action and to act charitably to help those so harmed.

Integrity is attributed to individuals and organizations that consistently act in accord with ethical principles. We rely on such individuals in our business transactions, and their good choices are anticipated by us so we trust these individuals and their organizations.

Trust, therefore, describes the relation between the stakeholders and individuals and their organizations who have acted with integrity. Of course, trust can be misplaced, and false trust is part of ethical failures.

Several stories reveal the importance of trust. Margaret's courage to act on her principles over a lifetime lead to trust by individuals, her company, the banking community and women

---

[1] Oliver F. Williams and Patrick E. Murphy, "The Ethics of Virtue: A Moral Theory for Marketing," *Journal of Macromarketing,* 10,1(Spring, 1990) 19-29; and Oliver F. Williams and Patrick E. Murphy, "A Moral Theory of Business," in *A Virtuous Life in Business,* Oliver F. Williams and John Houck, ed. (Rowman & Littlefield Publishers, Inc.: Lanham, Maryland, 1992).

in the general business community. The universal praise and respect for her made her story seem unreal to some readers. However, many told me her story, and I observed it myself.

Training managers goes beyond the classroom and is their everyday experience as they gain expertise and skills in making decisions and acting upon them. Corporate leaders need to ask themselves whether their companies' training incorporates an ethical dimension or excludes it. If they experience ethical failures in their day-to-day practice, the prospects are poor for ethical success in major matters.

HOW THE STORIES WERE COLLECTED

The stories were collected by asking executives to recall exemplary conduct that they had observed.[1] I never used the term, virtue or virtuous conduct in conducting the interviews but talked about exemplary behavior. Invariably, they interpreted 'exemplary' as 'ethical' or 'virtuous' conduct. Mostly, the recollections were about others, but sometimes they were about themselves. I asked them:

> 1. When you think about your business experience or your observation of the experience of others -- what conduct stands our in your mind as exemplary?
> 2. What happened?
> 3. What did you learn from it?

The questions were intended to get the executives to reflect on the executive and the episode(s). One to three hour interviews were tape recorded during which they told their stories. The interviews were transcribed, edited and returned

---

[1] The methodology was based on that developed by Morgan W. McCall, Jr., Michael M. Lombardo and Ann M. Morrison, *The Lessons of Experience: How Successful Executives Develop on the Job* (Lexington, Massachusetts, D.C.: Heath and Company, Lexington Books, 1988), pp. 191-194.

to the interviewees for their comment and approval. They were asked for any change, addition or deletion. Their comments were included and the interviews were re-edited as stories. Again, the interviewees had the opportunity to make changes, and their changes were incorporated into the stories.

Two approaches were used in collecting the stories. The first was to interview executives from different organizations, with the executives telling episodes about themselves or others. The second approach was to conduct six to ten interviews on one individual in the context of that person's organization.

In the first approach, we contacted 120 alumni of the University of Wisconsin-Milwaukee's Executive MBA Program and asked to interview them about exemplary conduct that they observed.[1] About 25 alumni executives agreed to relate episodes of exemplary conduct of which 19 actually had stories to relate. The other six included in the 25 offered their opinions on theories of ethics. The 95, who declined to relate stories of exemplary conduct, were interviewed briefly by telephone. They felt that they had no stories to contribute.

In addition to alumni, we contacted about two hundred members of the Milwaukee Chapter of the Financial Executives Institute; and fifteen executives responded with stories. Also several of the persons contacted referred me to others that they felt had episodes to relate.

My impression from talking to the "non-respondents" was that they found the story telling mode an awkward way of expressing themselves, and this may explain why some did not respond with episodes or stories. On the other hand, some executives felt the reason for the lack of stories was the self perception of the executives. They said that they saw their "doing the right thing" as ordinary conduct, not exemplary.

Alternatively, one could interpret the non-response as meaning that these executives had not observed exemplary conduct. For example, one responded, "I'm very sorry, but

---

[1] I gratefully acknowledge the substantial contribution of Dr. David McLain in designing the sample, contacting the alumni and conducting interviews with them.

unfortunately I have not witnessed or heard of any such action." The possibility that non-responding executives had not seen exemplary conduct can be inferred from data in another study. In this study, McCall and others found that only 20% of the key events in the careers of executives featured a specific person, with most key events featuring work assignments rather than people. They also found that 33% of significant bosses were remembered as having few redeeming virtues.[1]

The second approach focused on two persons who are recognized as exemplary leaders in their companies and communities. Both are retired. Executives in and out of their organizations were interviewed with the above questions rephrased to ask about these leaders. The interviews, lasting from one to three hours, were transcribed and edited to describe episodes and stories in their careers. Ten persons were interviewed for one leader , and six for the other -- resulting in six stories. The stories about one leader were:

Investing for Clients;
The Glass Ceiling;
Obligations to Clients;
Standing for Autonomy.
The stories about the other leader were:
Honesty as an Executive Style;
ESOP (Employee Stock Ownership Plans).

While the first set of interviews surveyed exemplary conduct across organizations, the second set looked at two leaders over the course of their careers within the context of their organizations. Considering how fragile virtue can be, depth is needed as well as breadth to see the unfolding of virtue.

The interviews are confidential because of the material discussed. Accordingly, names and identities are disguised including those of the storytellers, persons in the stories, companies, industries and places. There was one exception. The storyteller in "Principled Action" quoted published material about his grandfather, the protagonist in the story; and the

---

[1]McCall et al., op. cit., pp. 67-70.

cited material is referenced in the footnotes. The citation causes the name of the protagonist to be revealed, and this was approved by the storyteller.

The stories are grouped by the virtues that seem to pre-dominate the action, yet the groupings are only a rough cut for the action intertwines many dimensions of ethical conduct.

PART I

ADHERING TO THE LAW

Law, as an ideal, is linked to justice and a civil society. Hammurabi set forth a code of law in ancient times (about 2100 B.C.), and proclaimed this link, "I establish law and justice."[1] Moses urged the Hebrew people in his farewell address to follow the law so they would have life, "For this commandment which I command you this day is not too hard for you...See I have set forth before you this day [the choice between] life and good, death and evil.[2] Linking the law to justice and civility is a common theme in world religions, and people are urged to follow the Law.

Business men and women can strive to adhere to codes that include laws of government and moral codes of religion and the general culture, but their observance can extend beyond these codes. They also can adhere to their professional codes such as those in accounting or advertising, and they can adhere to the codes of their companies as well as to the basic code of free enterprise. Law is used here in the wider sense of the codes relevant for business decisions. The business people who told me their stories of exemplary conduct had to discern a fit with a blend government, moral and business codes. Their efforts were to interpret and adhere to law as reflected in this multiplicity of codes. The action in the stories usually involved one or two principles derived from this body of codes.

---

[1] *Robert Francis Harper. The Code of Hammurabi, King of Babylon..* 2nd ed. in John Bartlett, *Bartlett's Familiar Quotations* 13th ed. (Boston, 1982), p.3a.

[2] Deuteronomy: 30, 11-15. *The New Oxford Annotated Bible with the Apocrypha* (New York, Oxford University Press, 1973), p. 254.

In interpreting the body of codes, executives can find that the outcomes of specific actions may not be clear, whether they lead to a just and civil society. Also, one aspect of law may seem to conflict with other aspects; and the hierarchy of values in the law may seem ambiguous. So interpreting the law can be difficult.

In these circumstances, adherence to the law is a virtue. It is based on insight that a society's law achieves -- over the long pull -- civility and justice. The virtue is reflected in conduct that consistently follows law, as interpreted by conscience; and this virtue expresses trust that the law is the right way to live. The poet, Karl Shapiro, expressed the thought in an elegy to an American soldier, killed during the war.[1] Shapiro wrote that the soldier had cast his ballot although he distrusted those elected; but he had trusted in the law. Martin Luther said, "It is neither safe nor prudent to do aught against conscience. Here I stand -- I cannot do otherwise."[2]

There are seven stories in Part I: "Returning a Gift"; "Investing for Clients"; "Pressure from Above"; "Standing Alone"; "Accurate Reporting"; Blatant Violation"; and "Ambiguous Obligation"

RETURNING A GIFT

The storyteller's colleagues at work held a baby shower for him, and they invited a friend of his who was also a supplier to the company. The friend/vendor brought a gift (small value), but the storyteller did not want to accept the gift if it violated company policy. He tells what he did to see whether company policy applied and what his action was. In the process of striving to adhere to company policy he embarrassed his friend and apparently 'cooled' their relationship. He struggled between compassion and adherence to the law. In the end,

---

[1] Karl Shapiro, "Elegy for a Dead Soldier," in *Love & War: Art & God by Karl Shapiro*. (Stuart Wright, Publisher, 1984), p. 54.

[2] "Speech at the Diet of Worms," Bartlett op. cit., p. 86b.

he felt bound to adhere to the letter of the company's code even though it did not seem to be general practice of his superiors. Following the law was hard, and he had to trust that it was the right thing to do.

INVESTING FOR CLIENTS

The president of a trust company was under pressure not to terminate --literally overnight -- a loan to a major corporation. His company was a subsidiary of a holding company, and the holding company also had banking subsidiaries. The overnight loan was made by the trust company to the major corporation, but this corporation was also a customer of the holding company's banking subsidiaries. The holding company and its banking subsidiary feared that calling the loan overnight would harm their relation with the corporation. On the other hand, the president of the trust company believed that the law required him to consider only the interests of their clients whose money was being managed by the trust company. Accordingly, he called the loan overnight, and this information accidentally got into the hands of the financial community before the major corporation had an opportunity to prepare a statement. The trust president adhered to what he saw as right, but he had to consider the cost of his action.

PRESSURE FROM ABOVE

The storyteller is pressured by his boss to approve the payment of inflated expenses to a consulting firm, but the storyteller refused. His company had acquired a business, and the agreement called for paying $65 million to the owner in his home country and $10 million to the owner's consulting firm in Switzerland. The storyteller believed that the consulting firm was not equipped to undertake engagements worth the money so the engagements would need to be a sham. Taking tax deductions for the consulting fees as expenses would, therefore, be inappropriate in his mind. A struggle ensued, and the pressure on him was intense. He held his ground and was not fired, but his career was blocked at the company. The story relates what he did to protect himself. He had a successful career elsewhere after this incident, but he might have achieved fame and power with a career in one of the largest corporations if he had 'played ball' with his boss.

STANDING ALONE

A chief financial officer tells the story of a moral dilemma that he faced midway through his career. The company's net cash flow was decreasing but the demands for cash were increasing. Not only was the company becoming illiquid, but it faced the possibility of violating its bond covenant agreement. The storyteller recognized the need to restrict its uses of cash to maintain the necessary liquidity.

Because of the threatened illiquid condition, the board was to consider whether the dividend should be cut. The storyteller did an analysis of the situation and came to the conclusion that the dividend had to be reduced. He presented this to his boss, the CEO, who seemed to go along with it. Then he presented it to the board along with his recommendation. The CEO responded that the dividend should not be reduced; and in the ensuing debate the other directors split three to three, making the storyteller the seventh and pivotal vote.

The storyteller is faced with the moral dilemma: Should he do what he believed to be right and lose his influence (and possibly his position) in the company; or should he save his position by following the other directors and vote with the CEO, his boss. The story relates what he did.

ACCURATE REPORTING

A substantial sum was charged to a project for items that were for the personal use of two of the company's four owners. The controller, who was a young man at the time, had to decide what to do about this charge. The two owners told him not to worry about it -- leave it be. The controller felt that it was a misappropriation of assets, but he did not have the authority to change what had been charged to the project. He decided that he could not leave it be, but he had to do something.

A BLATANT VIOLATION

The chief financial officer(CFO) crossed swords with the chief executive officer(CEO) over the CEO's directive on the allocation and estimation (juggling?) of some costs. The story is told by the vice president of operations who sided with the CFO. The CFO and VP won the day because of some external events, but the CEO said it was a misunderstanding. The CFO and VP resigned some time later.

AMBIGUOUS OBLIGATIONS

The storyteller is the chief financial officer of a large company, and he described two decisions that he made for his company. The first involved making a payment under a lease. The second decision was the classification of assets to reduce the company's property taxes. In both cases, he had the opportunity to pay a lower or higher amount, depending on his interpretation of the situation. He paid a higher amount in one instance and the lower amount in the other. The CFO explains his decisions in the story.

RETURNING A GIFT

"When I was interviewed for my initial position at my company, I was told that employees should not accept gifts in any manner or fashion from a vendor. The interviewer gave me this example from his own experience: The interviewer had received flowers from a local florist, and he asked the florist to take them back -- and they were. The interviewer, I believe, was telling me that accepting gifts was not to be tolerated, no matter how insignificant.

"My department gave me a baby shower, and they invited an outside consultant whose business with the company was my responsibility. He brought a gift to the party; and, unfortunately, I had not told him to bring nothing. It was an awkward situation because the gift was worth only a few dollars.

"I followed up and sought advice. Nobody had ever codified what to do in these circumstances although the company's written policy is to accept nothing of any value. I went through the process of consulting my boss and somebody in the legal department. The legal person asked me if I felt there was anything wrong with it. I said that I didn't know and that was why I was calling. My boss had no opinion on the matter, but I interpreted the manual as saying that accepting a gift of any value was not to be tolerated.

"It is somewhat insulting to tell some one who brought a small gift to the party that his action was not appropriate and the gift should perhaps be given to charity. The upshot was that I asked him to take back the gift. I tried to do it privately so as not to cause embarrassment to the consultant. He really did not understand why I refused the gift. This kind of cracked our relationship, but I did it because it was the right thing to do."

STUDY QUESTIONS

"Returning a Gift" was a situation that occurred in a Fortune 100 company. The company had an extensive code of ethics that applied to multiple locations. The storyteller worked at the headquarters of the subsidiary, and the corporate headquarters was in a distant city. Although the code was corporate-wide, its implementation was decentralized.

The storyteller seemed to struggle with balancing his feelings of compassion for his friend and commitment to adhering to the corporate code of ethics. He was also concerned with the consequences for his friendship of returning the gift.

1. Was the storyteller being stiff necked in returning the gift and giving less weight to his friend's feelings? Should he give more weight to his sense of compassion? Why or why not?

2. The purpose of law is to achieve justice and civility. What does justice and civility demand in this situation?

3. Is adherence to the corporate code a virtue when the amount is several dollars?

4. Should the storyteller follow a stricter interpretation of the ethics code than his superiors? They did not say that the code required him to return the gift.

5. The storyteller simply seemed to be following his conscience. Does that justify his action? Are there situations where managers must be more flexible in balancing their own interpretations of right and wrong with the judgments of their associates?

INVESTING FOR CLIENTS[1]

The chief executive of a Trust Company told this story about her predecessor and mentor. The law required, in her view, a 'Chinese wall' between banking decisions and trust decisions. Investment decisions for trust accounts were to be made solely on the basis of the interests of the clients even when this created turbulence for banking relationships. The chief executive said that her predecessor forcefully made this point on a number of occasions.

In one episode there was conflict between the Trust Company's investment decisions and the holding company's interest in banking relations. The Trust Company has arrangements to invest their clients' cash in demand notes of major companies for very short periods of time. These are notes from 15 to 50 million dollars. The Trust Company monitors the credit worthiness of these companies very closely. Serious concern can lead to terminating the relationship. Usually the Trust Company would give 30 days notice before it no longer invested in a company's demand notes.

On one occasion, the Trust Company did not feel that they could wait 30 days and the notes were redeemed overnight. The company was an important customer of the holding company's banking operations, but her predecessor took the position that, once the Investment Committee made the decision to terminate the note because of question about the firm's credit worthiness, it had to be terminated in all of its clients' accounts at the same time. The termination could not be phased by terminating the note in several accounts at a time for that would not adhere to their understanding of the law.

---

[1] This story is about the mentor of the person who is the protagonist in "The Glass Ceiling", "Obligations to Clients" and "Standing for Autonomy".

The news of the decision to redeem the notes reached the financial community before that customer could prepare a statement. So the strain was compounded, and the customer was "furious". Understandably the management of the holding company "had a fit".

A manager said, "He was right, he knew he was right; he knew that we were charged with the responsibility of managing that money for our clients so there was no way he was going to change his mind. No one was going to convince him that the association should continue between the Trust Company and the company selling the demand notes because of other business relationships with the holding company's banking operations." The episode characterized her predecessor's courage in adhering to the law in her eyes.

STUDY QUESTIONS

1. Usually the Trust Company gave 30 day notice before terminating a relationship, but it did not do so for the company described in the story. It was a major corporation; the holding company management was "furious" about the overnight cancellation by the Trust Company; and the banking arm wanted to continue their relationship with this major company and thought the cancellation would hurt their relationship. Would it have been better for the Trust Company to give the 30 day notice even though the company fell below the Trust Company's criteria for credit worthiness?

2. The company did, in fact, turn around; and it is a very successful business today. The chief executive's predecessor must have recognized this possibility, yet he did not let the prospect of losing an important client govern his decision. He saw a Chinese wall between his actions in the trust company and what happened 'across the street' in the holding company's banking operations. What would you have done?

3. Adhering to the law -- 'being a stickler' -- is not popular. What is the case for consistently adhering to the law (and corporate code)?

PRESSURE FROM ABOVE

"My rise through the echelons of the company was steady. Eventually, I became CEO of its Medical Instrumentation Group.[1] Shortly after the appointment, I learned of a major deficiency in the product line.

"I flew to Europe to see Felix who was a multibillionaire owner of a gigantic consortium of electronic companies. One of the companies produced equipment that we badly needed in our product line. We met in his vast office, largest I've ever seen. After explaining that we would like to buy 70,000 units each year for five years, I added that we would really like to buy the entire subsidiary.

"Felix said, 'My sixtieth birthday was last month. In my country, when a man in my position reaches his sixtieth birthday, he calls his closest advisors and friends together and considers what he should do with his assets, what his future should be.' After a pause, he continued, 'They advised me that I should sell the subsidiary you want. Now you walk in the door. Maybe it's an omen. I think I will sell it to you, if I can get my price, of course.'

"Elated, I returned to corporate headquarters and reported this to Marty, my boss. We then obtained approval from the president of the company to negotiate with Felix. Marty later achieved fame as the head of another conglomerate. He was a skillful negotiator with incredible stamina.

"The negotiations dragged on for about three months with meetings in several European cities. From time to time I participated, but I had operations to run. Marty and the lawyers did most of it -- particularly the last couple of weeks.

"Finally both sides agreed to a price of $75 million cash to be paid over a span of three years, interest free. Felix insisted that $65 million be paid in his country's currency. The other

---

[1] Names in the story are fictitious.

$10 million be paid in Swiss francs to a consulting firm he owned in Switzerland. The money was for consulting services to our Medical Instrumentation operations. This way we would get the money into Switzerland under a favorable tax arrangement that he had. Our company would get a tax deduction in the United States with the $10 million treated as a business expense.

"I knew nothing of the arrangement, only that the deal had been made for $75 million in cash. After the celebration that followed the signing of the deal, Marty explained the deal to me and said, 'You have to use $10 million in consulting fees over the next three years.'

"Shocked, I pointed out the enormity of that amount. He was adamant. Then I learned the consulting firm had a staff of only five people -- all accountants, lawyers, and clerks. Not a one knew anything about electronics. Again, I protested to Marty but was told to comply.

'I balked. I began a diary of Marty's directions, orders, explanations, exhortations, and eruptions -- and my objections. For example, Marty said that I should collect industrial statistics, send them to Geneva, and let them send them back to me with a bill, maybe with some new charts, or graphs, or analyses. I resisted.

"Marty ordered me to let the consulting firm handle all travel arrangements so they could mark up travel costs. Again, I wouldn't do it.

"I continued to write it all down in my diary.

"Felix was raising hell about me to Marty so I agreed to take a trip to London on one of Felix's Learjets. He had a fleet of airplanes, some Learjets, all legally owned by the consulting firm. I was reluctant to do this because of my sermons to my managers and staff about frugality. I had always set the example, riding in the back of the airplane. Now I took a private plane; and, to put salt in my wounds, the bill for the trip was $5,000! I erupted and swore I'd never use one of Felix's planes again, and I ordered my people not to do so.

"Marty insisted on 100% loyalty, or you were on his blacklist forever. I had been close to him for several years. I ran his largest operation. We traveled together extensively, had philosophized, and bonded over exchanges of stories of combat in the big war. I thought we were good friends.

"Now he became extremely cool, often testy and brusque with me. Despite this, I continued to refuse to cooperate because it was contrary to my understanding of tax law.

"After six months of these incidents, Marty was promoted to be a group executive, and I was the logical successor. I didn't get the promotion. I believe that Marty put the 'kibosh' on it.

"My new boss was about five years younger than me. I'd known him for a long time and had a good relationship with him. I immediately explained the problem to him. I said, 'I've had big problems with Marty over this, and I hope I'm not going to have trouble with you. You should know that I'm not going to use that phony consulting firm for anything.'

"All this was news to him. He said he'd talk to the company president and get back to me. About a week later, he called and said, 'Forget about the consulting firm.'

"I learned later that -- because I wouldn't cooperate -- the company told Felix that it would pay his consulting firm $5 million in Swiss francs and not take a deduction in the U.S. as a business expense -- The net cost to our company was the same, but Felix had only $5 million going to Switzerland at a favorable tax rate instead of $10 million.

"I understand that Felix exploded. Our company said that I would not cooperate nor let my people cooperate. So that was the end of it as far as the company was concerned.

"Felix could do nothing because the entire amount should have been paid into his country, and none should have been paid into Switzerland. Any lawsuit against our company would have exposed the scheme, putting him into deep trouble in his own country. He signed an amendment to the price, and I heard that he was fuming.

"I expected the ax to fall on me.

"Nothing happened. The then chief financial officer told me confidentially that they were all scared of me. I knew too much, and was on the side of the angels.

"I believe that I would probably have been left to take the brunt of the blame if I had participated in the scheme and if it had fallen apart. But now, if I blew the whistle, some executives would have been in trouble, but not me.

"I had job security!

"Marty left the company to become the CEO of another company that he built into a gigantic organization. He achieved considerable fame, being the subject of articles in major business publications.

"I also departed the company and became the CEO of another company in a part of the country that was much more conservative in its business practices."

I asked the storyteller how it turned out.

"He said, "Well, if you fast forward about fifteen years from the time the company acquired Felix's subsidiary, there was a lot of trouble.

"The manager of Felix's consulting firm was charged with a violation of the home country's tax law -- he was a citizen of that country. So he made a deal. He told them about the arrangement that Felix had made with my former company to divert $10 million into Switzerland that should have been paid into Felix's home country and taxed there.

"The home country's tax people investigated; and they soon informed my former company that they appeared guilty of conspiracy to defraud the home country of tax revenue. The home country's tax people told the company that they would not pursue conspiracy charges if they paid Felix the extra $10 million due on the original deal into the home country.

"Both my former company and Felix said that the price had been reduced $5 million because the company discovered deficiencies in various assets. They both insisted that there had never been a consulting agreement. Evidently, the original agreement with the consulting firm didn't mention consulting, only that $10 million would be paid to the consulting firm over three years. Although it was the company's intent to take a deduction for bogus consulting services, they couldn't be proved unless some one from the company admitted it.

"The company's attorney came to see me. After pleasantries and reminiscences, I handed him a typed copy of the notes that I had kept in my diary. As he read them, I could see his face becoming paler; I thought that he might faint."

"He said, 'Felix's home country can't prove a thing without these notes. With them, they'd blow us out of the water. Because of the dollar's fall against the home currency, it would cost us $7.5 million instead of the original $5 million.'

"I shrugged and said nothing.

"The company attorney said, 'You could put Felix and Marty in jail. At the very least, you'd ruin their reputations. The scandal could cost Marty his job.'

"I don't want to hurt anybody, I said. I'm not that kind of guy. But 15 years ago, both of those guys made my life miserable. I think they hurt me too.

"I let that sink in for a moment, then continued. All I want is for you to tell them that I could hurt them big right now if I wanted to, but I won't. And tell them that I am putting the diary in safe custody with instructions to send it to tax people in Felix's home country along with the whole story if anything happens to me. And copies will go to the major business publications.

"Felix's home country dropped the case against my former company for lack of evidence. They made an undisclosed settlement with Felix.

"Felix died a few years ago. Marty has never forgiven me for disobeying him. I'm told that he hates me. Well, as somebody once said, I'm proud of my friends, and I'm proud of my enemies.'"

STUDY QUESTIONS

1. What price did the storyteller pay for his adherence to his understanding of the tax law. What price did his boss, Marty, and their company pay?

2. Was adherence worth the price or should the storyteller have gone along with the deal? What would you have done? How would you rationalize Marty's point of view.

3. Why should the storyteller resist inflated fees for services from Felix's consulting firm, such as travel-ing on planes in the firm's private fleet? It would have allowed his company to implement the agreement with the consulting firm. Was it wrong?

4. The storyteller's diary seemed to be important in protecting the storyteller from retribution. From the very beginning, what were the signs that led the storyteller to keep a diary. Under what circumstances would you keep a diary about your business activity.

STANDING ALONE

"This was a tough situation all the way through. My boss was a very interesting person -- bright, articulate, and volatile. He and I got on dandy for probably the first year, but then there began a series of issues. The company was involved in expanding, using its financial resources to build a new business. I was the chief financial officer.

"The company's basic business was very, very liquid. The buyer paid advance fees so the more business you had, the more liquid you were. Also, you got additional moneys when you started the contract. Then, when you paid suppliers' bills, you paid on 30-day terms, but you got your receipts on 10-day terms. So it was a nice business from that standpoint.

"The new business was just the opposite. It was very heavily capital intensive. The company soon absorbed its cash flow in the new business, and it became apparent that its earnings were diminishing. So the financial position reversed from being very liquid to being threatened with a lack of liquidity.

"Well, I had recently been elected to the board, and this was my second meeting. The issue before the board was what we should do about the dividend. Would the cash flow support it and our ongoing business needs. Continuing the dividend would have violated the covenants in our bond indenture agreement.

"So I made my case the best I could that we should not continue the dividend. Everybody listened. My boss spoke up after I gave my talk at the initial meeting and said, 'Well I guess that settles it.' Everybody was quiet when he spoke up. He seemed really impressed initially. It seemed to me that the discussion ended and the issue was about settled.

"Well, my boss was a major shareholder; and I did not realize at first how important the dividend was to him. After commenting that my analysis settled the issue, he made the case for continuing the dividend -- that the shareholders needed a regular dividend.

I had talked to him before the meeting about the dividend and the covenants. Of course he was not one to sit down for any extended period of time. He did not necessarily agree with me, but he didn't disagree either in our earlier conversation. It was left hanging there. In fact we also discussed the academic point on the connection between value of the stock, future cash flow, and the covenant.

"Now the board was in a little bit of a dilemma after he spoke for continuing the dividend. There were seven directors present. Three outside directors agreed that we ought not to pay the dividend or, at least, ought to reduce it measurably. Three inside directors -- including my boss -- wanted to continue the dividend.

"I was the seventh director so everybody turned to me. I was really stressed. I hadn't thought that things would turn out like this. Here I am -- having to choose between what I would consider to be my responsible fiduciary behavior on the one hand, and voting with my boss who hired me, put me on the board, and was the fellow I had to deal with every day. So I tried to see whether we couldn't discuss the issue a little further, rather than just my voting one way or the other. We looked at the issue from different parameters, but the vote was still the same. Finally my boss said, 'Look, which way are you going to vote?'

"I decided I better opt against continuing the dividend at the present level. It was something that I felt that I had to do. I had to establish a certain amount of independent credibility -- financial fiduciary responsibility.

"That was the way that the vote went -- against continuing the dividend at its current level; but my boss saw to it that the meeting was not adjourned indefinitely, but was left open to reconvene the next day.-- that was a rarity. One of the outside directors, who favored reducing or eliminating the dividend left that evening. That night the boss had gotten additional ammunition and had convinced the two remaining outside directors to vote his way. Overnight, probably, the more he thought about it, the more he thought that he needed the money.

"The next day, I became a minority of one and that's tough! I still voted the same way, but the remaining outside directors voted with my boss. It was an awkward situation, and I felt very pressured, a tough situation.

"Our relationship did not change immediately. We never spoke of the position I took at that board meeting. He never indicated dissatisfaction with my vote. He liked to go out and sell. He was a wonderful salesman. He told me, 'You take care of the business; I'll go out and draw first blood.' It's hard to understand exactly what he meant, and I did not fully understand what he meant. But at least he wanted to be free of the administrative chores. He didn't want to be bothered with budgeting, oversight of the finances, talking with bankers and so forth. He was glad to leave that to me. It was unusual for me to find my self in disagreement with him at that time.

"Our relationship grew more strained after a while, and I began to find myself in disagreement with him more often. He felt free to yell, to direct his explosive personality at me. But that is not uncommon for him. He did that pretty commonly among a whole group of people. But I had to do what was financially sound -- establish a certain amount of independent credibility despite our relationship. Later events triggered my resignation from the firm."

STUDY QUESTIONS

1. What does the story imply about the storyteller's professional code of conduct?

2. Should he have adhered to this code when he was the only one voting against his boss' position by the second day of the board's meeting?

3. He tried to resolve the differences among board members, but finally was forced to vote. This put him in a position of adhering to the law and jeopardizing

his career or backing his boss and gaining more power within the company. Is it fair to expect the storyteller to jeopardize his career for the sake of strictly adhering the law and one's professional code?

4. Corporate officers are often elected to the board and are called 'inside directors'. They face the possibility that the storyteller faced. Circumstances may arise where they will need to choose between voting what they think is right or voting to support their boss, the CEO. Would it be better for them not to serve on the their boards to avoid this moral dilemma? Or should they simply take their chances to gain the advantages of serving on their boards?

ACCURATE REPORTING

"When I was a relatively young man, I was a controller for a large construction company that was owned by four people. Two were engineering type people who worked there, and two were law partners and absentee owners.

"One day, going through some accounting on one of our major jobs, I found a lot of unusual charges that related to lawn tractors and snow throwers. They were purchased by the two on-site owners and being charged against this job. I really felt that it was improper and talked to the people who were the recipients of these unusual transactions. They told me not to worry about it.

I didn't really feel that was the right thing to do so, after some soul searching, I talked to a local priest. It turned out that I decided I had to do something. I ended up calling the two absentee owners and making an appointment -- documenting what I had and giving it to them. Then I immediately went back to the office and told the other two what I had done.

"They were very unhappy, but after a week or so it was blown over. I think they respected me for it. I think to this day -- although one of them is now dead -- they all thought better of me. It was a very trying time, but it seemed to work out well."

I asked the storyteller whether they threatened to fire him or harm him. He said, "No, nothing like that. I think that I must have put the two on-site owners in a rather embarrassing position where they really couldn't have done that -- though, they technically owned control of the firm between them. It probably wasn't the worst strategy, doing what I thought I had to do and then telling them I did it"

I asked the storyteller what considerations went through his head when he decided that he had to do something. "Well, I just felt that they were misappropriating assets from the other shareholders -- they weren't getting lawn tractors; they weren't getting snow throwers. These were not small pieces of equipment. They had a large multiple of thousands of dollars. They were being hidden in a job for a client somewhere out in the state. I just didn't think it was right. It was my obligation to point out that this charge was being made.

"I talked to the on-site owners. The equipment was delivered to their homes. It was not an oversight, nor a clerical error, nor anything like that. They said, 'don't worry about it'; but I was obliged not to let this be. I talked to them and gave them the chance to correct it.

"I learned from this that you have to do what has to be done. You have to bite the bullet."

STUDY QUESTIONS

1. The on-site owners told the storyteller not to worry about what costs were charged to what projects. Would you have worried?

2. The storyteller felt that he had an obligation to point out that this charge was being made. Do you agree? Disagree?

3. What risk did the storyteller take? Would you have taken this risk?

A BLATANT VIOLATION

"We had a sister company where we had an arm's-length relationship. We were the operations end. We manufactured the product. They were the sales and distribution end. The arrangement was that we manufactured the product, passed along the product to our sales and distribution sister company at a standard cost. The product was then sold, and the two companies split the profits. It was more or less an evergreen situation. They couldn't work with anyone else on this product. We couldn't work with anybody else. We were kind of permanently joined.

"I came along when there was a change in the ownership of the production company, as did the CEO and other senior managers. So we were all coming into a relatively new situation.

"We had come in and done some things from an operational standpoint to save the company a significant amount of money. We were looking at savings of a million dollars on one particular program.

"We examined how the company had been running. It had been very, very cash rich. The former management had no need to necessarily manage it, from an optimization standpoint. They were making more money than the owner could spend. So there was no need to fine tune the organization. We identified some opportunities. As I said, we were able to save a million dollars on a program.

"The new ownership invested a lot of money in buying it; and, besides, they had leveraged the company. Understandably, they expected the new senior management to generate a high financial return. We were 'hired guns', and did not hold a significant ownership position.

"The CEO decided that we were not going to share this information about the cost savings with our sister company. We were going to pass the product along at the old standard cost -- not the new correct costs. He said we would not share the savings because we earned it. He said that we did things smarter, better than the old management team; and why should we be sharing these benefits? He said that since the savings were the result of our efforts, we should not have to share them with the sister company.

"Again, the sister companies -- manufacturing and marketing -- were entirely separate with different ownership's. All the agreements that were structured between the companies were such that the true costs were going to be shared.

"The chief financial officer (CFO) refused to go ahead and do it. He argued that it was a blatant violation of our contract. The auditors would catch it when they came through and looked at the books. the CFO did not believe that we could hide the costs. I [vice president of operations] supported him in his position. The CEO argued that the auditors would not catch the 'juggling' to inflate our costs. He said that we could take a chance.

"If something came to light -- where we were in violation of the original agreements -- it could create absolute chaos in terms of the overall relationship. So from a financial standpoint, the cost-risk/benefit -- what we had to gain versus what we had to lose -- it didn't make economic sense. But at a higher level, it wasn't right. If things had unraveled, you could jeopardize the entire relationship. It could have jeopardized the viability of the business. It was that serious.

"The discussion among us did not reach a resolution because something else happened. A member of our board of directors resigned and ended up on the board of the sister company. He knew what was being planned; but, as far as I know, was not part of the discussion and had not given an opinion. Since he knew about the cost saving, we had to open up and share the information with the sister company. Our CEO now stated that we were going to do this all along.

"Later, both the CFO and I resigned. I did not think that the CEO could be trusted. I not only questioned his ethical standards but also his business judgment."

STUDY QUESTIONS

1. What were the arguments presented by the CEO not to share the saving with the sister company? Was there an ethical principle or virtue involved?

2. What were the arguments of the CFO and the VP of operations? What were the ethical principles or virtues involved?

3. Compare these arguments. Who was right?

4. Did the CFO and VP of operations take unnecessary risk by opposing the CEO? They wanted the cost saving shared with the sister company, and that happened because of other events, not their discussions with the CEO.

5. The VP of operations did not know of any connection between the CEO's intent to keep the cost savings and the move of the board member from the manufacturing company to the marketing company. Could there have been one? Describe a possible scenario involving this connection.

6. Compare this story with the story, "Accurate Reporting". In both stories, the protagonists had to decide between adhering to their professional code of conduct with possible career opportunities. What other virtues would be brought into play?

AMBIGUOUS OBLIGATIONS

The chief financial officer (CFO) told me that he follows different standards when his obligation is clear from when it is unclear. He told me how he handled both situations.

"One situation was a matter of a lease for a warehouse facility that my company has. The terms of the lease include our paying all utilities, taxes and insurance related to the facility. However, we don't pay 100% of the taxes for the property where the facility is located. There are other buildings on the property that are not leased by us so we pay a proportion of the real estate taxes that is determined by a formula, stated in the lease. The formula requires that we pay 60% of any increase in real estate taxes over the last twelve years. We calculated that we owed $24000 for real taxes to the landlord.

"The property had been sold, and the new owners informed us that we owed $4000 -- $20000 less than our calculation. We could have just paid the $4000 and then see if anything comes of it later on. Instead we notified them that we calculated a much higher tax liability and requested that they check their calculations. It took them awhile. I don't think they had the information available right away. After going back to the lease and probably getting a copy of the base period tax bill, they arrived at the same amount we did. So we paid the $24000.

"This was a straight forward decision. It was clear what we owed under the terms of the lease, and it would have been wrong to pay a smaller amount simply because they made a mistake and maybe were unaware of the error. It would have been wrong to take advantage of that mistake. Under the terms of the lease, we agreed to pay $24000; and we should make a payment of $24000. We would have been taking $20000 from them. So we would have been doing something against not only our word, but what we agreed to in a written contract."

I asked the CFO whether he consulted with the CEO or others in the organization. He said, "No, it was clear. It was a black and white case in which it was absolutely true that we should pay them $24000. I do think that our standards within the company are such that other people would have done the same thing or expected me to do what I did. There was no need to ask the president or anyone else what I should do.

"The other situation involves property taxes, and the tax obligation is not as clear. In this case, we are dealing with property taxes or machinery and equipment. Machinery and equipment is exempt if it is part of the manufacturing process; otherwise it is taxable as personal property.

"The state laws are very complex and there are cases and cases where machinery and equipment are taxable or exempt. We are advised by specialists in this area -- consultants and attorneys -- but, in the end, the company, itself, must make the decision because we complete the returns.

"It can be ambiguous how a piece of equipment should be classified. It may perform functions related to the manufacturing process, and it may perform other functions. I can create a pretty good picture how the equipment can be viewed one way, qualifying it to be tax exempt. But there is enough leeway, that it can be viewed another way. One assessor or somebody working for the state tax office might view it one way, and another assessor or official in the same state tax department might view it another way -- depending on how it is presented.

"In cases like that I feel it is my ethical responsibility to the company to give the interpretation that minimizes its taxes. I don't have any pangs of conscious and say, 'Oh, no, maybe I should look at it and divide it half way. I guess, in my mind, it's very, very clear that I should do everything I can to minimize taxes without being fraudulent. Anything that I think could qualify as tax exempt -- I classify as tax exempt."

I asked the CFO what was the difference between the two cases. He said, "There are a couple of differences. In the case of the lease, there was no ambiguity. It was clear that we had an obligation. In the case of the personal property taxes, there is significant room for interpretation. The first case was clear, while the second case was not clear -- left room for various interpretations.

"In minimizing taxes, I still feel that we are paying our just dues to the government so we are paying a fair share. But I wonder, if in my own mind-set, am I really saying that there is something wrong with taxes? Not that I don't recognize the government's need for taxes, and our obligation to pay taxes. It almost seems like it's everybody's job to try to push the obligation on to somebody else. You can see that in legislation there is a constant push and pull over what groups are going to pay and what groups will receive benefits. The ethical code for paying taxes is different from that for meeting contract obligations.

"In the case of the contract, there was an obligation to pay what was clearly and unambiguously called for. In the case of property taxes, there was no obligation to classify equipment and machinery as taxable when it could reasonably be interpreted to qualify as tax exempt."

STUDY QUESTIONS

1. Do you agree with the CFO that he had an obligation to point out that the landlord was undercharging the company? Explain.

2. Do you agree with the CFO that he does not have an obligation to point out to the revenue agent the increase in taxes? (The increase would result from a more strict interpretation of what machinery and equipment is taxable.)

3. The CFO applied a code of paying one's debts in the case of the lease, and he applied a code of minimizing one's taxes in the case about exemptions for machinery and equipment. Do these situations call for the same code? If so, which one? If not, why are different codes justified?

4. What action would you take in these situations?

5. Compare this story with "Principled Action. Both stories describe incidents where the storyteller believed that his company had an obligation to make payment to another organization even though that organization was unaware that a payment should be made. Payment was made in "Ambiguous Obligations" but not in "Principled Action". Can the different outcomes be justified? Not justified?

Part II

AVOIDING HARM

"Avoiding Harm" is the negative or 'do-not' side of the golden rule: "And as you wish that others would do to you, do so to them."[1] Avoiding harm is to not act in ways where you would be hurt if others acted in those ways toward you. This virtue calls for not doing what is prohibited in codes such as the moral laws given to Moses[2] -- e.g., falsely gaining possession of another's property. The virtue is intended to insure minimal justice.

Avoiding harm may seem to be a simple and straight forward rule to follow, but it is not. Even recognizing harm can be hard to do. The executive has to look at the multiplicity of codes to know what can be harmful in a given situation. Is it harmful to reduce the dividend for example?

Putting together actions that avoid harm may not be feasible; so executives are then faced with what harm they must do and what harm they must avoid. Recognizing harm and seeking to avoid it becomes a matter of judgment. Business men and women are left with discerning the right course and having the courage to act accordingly.

This is the opposite of the moral advice in Hinduism's Gita. Here, Krishna advised the Prince, Arjuna, to focus on the action and to be detached from the harm done. The Prince is not to seek the fruits (good and bad consequences) of his action but live in the struggle itself.[3]

---

[1]Luke 6: 31, *The New Oxford Annotated Bible*, op. cit., p. 1251.

[2]Exodus 20: 1-17, Ibid., 92.

[3]John Dunne. *The Way of All the Earth: Experiments in Truth and Religion.* (New York: The Macmillan Company, 1972) pp. 6 and 148.

Part II has five stories: "The Open Drawer"; "Justice and Generosity"; Justice and Honesty"; "Limits to Avoiding Harm"; and "Blow the Whistle".

THE OPEN DRAWER

The first story, "The Open Drawer", is a simple story about side payments. Both the company making the purchase and its supplier can be harmed if their agents have a kick-back arrangement between themselves. The storyteller describes two salesmen that he met at a convention. The successful one tells how he drops money in the purchasing manager's open drawer, commenting to the storyteller, "...that is how you do business." The less successful salesman does not engage in this practice, and the storyteller wonders how one balances one's survival and the harm to business. The amount of money in the story is small; but the same issue, with large amounts of money, confronts many businesses. The salesman and purchasing manager did not avoid harm to their companies, but they justified their side payment as the way business is done.

JUSTICE AND GENEROSITY

The second story on avoiding harm, "Justice and Generosity", is complex and is about payment for up-front work before sales are made. In many situations, the supplier does not charge for this work, but the costs are included in the price of the product or service if a sale is made. So the vendor covers this cost only if the transaction occurs -- even though the up-front work can be of substantial benefit to the potential buyer. The story is about the design of data systems, but the same arrangements occur for product design and testing.

The issue is balancing the interests of the supplier and the buyer. The vendor benefits from a sale but may be harmed by the cost of 'free' information if the sale is not realized. The buyer may be harmed from purchasing products or services without clear information but can benefit by using the supplier's information to make a purchase elsewhere. Once the buyer has the up-front information from a supplier, the buyer can negotiate a lower price from another supplier because it excludes the cost of generating the up-front information.

The story tells how executives for the supplier and the buyer dealt with this issue to avoid harm and to be fair to each other. Their virtuous actions reflect an archetype on good business relations -- but perhaps at a higher cost to the buyer. The protagonist is the senior vice president for the bank. The supplier did substantial up-front work for the bank, and the storyteller said that the senior vice president was prepared to pay the supplier for the work. However the supplier did not expect or ask for compensation, figuring that they had to "take their lumps" since the deal fell through.

The senior vice president then went beyond the bounds of avoiding harm and being fair. He was generous in his response. He gave the supplier the opportunity to enter a new line of business even though another firm with the expertise could have done the work for the bank. Being generous is not something one expects, perhaps, in business relations; but the story suggests that it has a place.

JUSTICE AND HONESTY

The story is about how customers treat work done by a supplier before there is an agreement on terms of purchase. It raises the issues of whether the customer should use this work without compensating the supplier and whether the supplier should withhold information to insure compensation for up-front work. The storyteller describes how his company tries to be fair and honest while dealing with companies that they consider to be unscrupulous. The story raises issues similar to "Justice and Generosity", but the outcomes are different.

LIMITS TO AVOIDING HARM

The storyteller distinguished where it is unacceptable to harm a customer and where he is acceptable. He described a situation where the customer went into Chapter 11, and the storyteller's company lost $50,000 that the customer owed them. The storyteller felt that the customer harmed him, and his allegiance and duty to the customer was negated as a consequence. The storyteller 'bad mouthed' the customer and sought to steer business away from them. He felt that it was acceptable to harm the customer in this way after what the customer had done to him.

At the same time, the storyteller described how he turned down business from a would-be buyer and referred the buyer to a competitor because he felt that the buyer would get a better deal from the competitor. He sought to provide the best price/product deal for the buyer, and his product had more exacting specifications and a higher price than the customer needed. He acted this way out of allegiance to the customer and the maintenance of a long term business relationship.

BLOW THE WHISTLE?

The storyteller's company was seeking a substantial order from a customer; and the customer's manager in charge of buying asked the storyteller's company for a kickback. They refused, but they also had to decide whether they should report the buyer's action to his company. The story described the subsequent events.

THE OPEN DRAWER

"I met two salesmen at a national sales managers meeting in South Carolina. One fellow was shabbily dressed and looked helter-skelter, but he seemed like a nice guy. He felt strongly that honesty was good business. He said that he tried to do the right thing and be upright in his business dealings. He never gave money under the table to get business. Still he was able to do business, he said, and was getting by.

"The other fellow flew to the meeting in his own plane. He was well dressed, very sharp and also seemed like a nice guy. After a very pleasant dinner, I hesitated then asked him: Here are two guys from the same city, seemingly different (and I described the first guy to him). How do you account for the difference. I knew it was an awkward question to ask somebody, but it was that point in the evening where it was OK, and he could just laugh and brush the question aside if he wanted.

"He smiled, 'Well, I'll tell you something about business. When I go to get a printing job from somebody, the buyer may open his desk drawer. I stand over the desk to fill out paper work; and, as I stoop over the desk, I drop an envelope into the drawer. The amount of money that's in the envelope depends on size of the printing job. What happens? I pay a guy $500. When the job is done, I tack $500 on to the final invoice and just call it 'additional proof reading' or whatever it may be. The printing buyer's company pays the total bill.

"The buyer is ahead $500; I'm ahead with my commission; my company is ahead with the added business; and his company gets a good printing job. No one is the wiser because the printing buyer approved the invoice and said that everything is OK.

"Obviously, it's a form of kickback. The guy who flew his airplane said, 'Well, that's the way we do business in my area.' He is successful. Is the other guy? The shabby guy said that he doesn't drop anything into a buyer's open desk drawer, and he said that he doesn't get that work either. Now that's the tough part.

"That was seven years ago, and companies are getting tougher on enforcing codes of conduct. Still you have to ask, 'Does honesty count? The shabby guy -- he's ethical; and he's suffering for it. Maybe he feels better."

STUDY QUESTIONS

1. At issue is whether the successful salesman is misappropriating his company's property. Would the price for the company making the purchase be lower if there were no side payment? If so, is the company's property being misappropriated?

2. The same question can be asked about the printing company. Would its costs be lower if there were no side payments? If so, is its property being misappropriated?

3. The successful salesman believes that this is the practice of the industry in his geographic area. Does the practice of the industry justify the action?

4. Does the story imply that the companies' managers knew about this practice? Is it acceptable to make the side payment if they do know? If they do not know?

5. The storyteller contrasted the two salesmen -- one making substantial income and the other just 'getting by.' The less successful salesman said that he was doing 'the right thing.' The storyteller asked whether honesty counted. Can the 'shabby' salesman expect to be successful when he refused to make side payments and 'do the right thing'?

6. Is success in business linked to exemplary conduct? Or is business rewarded for not being virtuous?

JUSTICE AND GENEROSITY

"I'm not sure how to characterize this story. I guess I'll leave that to you. The story spanned a couple of years, almost two decades ago. At the time we were just getting into the business of electronic funds transfer. We were a subsidiary of a company in heavy industry while we provided services -- computer information processing and software.

"I got a call from a major regional bank that held the dominant share in its retail market. It was a very, very strong bank. They were interested in a piece of software that we were marketing. For the bank this could represent a quarter to a half million dollar investment in their launching a new business. It could mean a $300,000 sale on our part. It clearly was a decision that would be visible to the bank's board. It was a large ticket expenditure.

"These folks called up and expressed an interest. We entered into some very serious discussions, led by my boss and the Vice Chairman of the bank. The bank decided to purchase our system and install it themselves. In the course of the discussion, the bank's staff became pretty well acquainted with us; and we, with them. My boss developed a solid business relation with the Vice Chairman. The Vice Chairman was a very decent fellow, probably in his early sixties. He retired not long after the conclusion of this story.

"We had negotiated an agreement over a period of weeks and were at the point of signing it. Work had begun in anticipation of executing this agreement. We were six months into our discussions with the bank.

At this point my boss and I were asked to come to their headquarters. We flew out there at their first open date. The Vice Chairman took us to dinner that evening along with a couple of his associates. They told us that the bank had made a change in its strategic direction, and their computer services was being organized as a separate subsidiary. So they were not going ahead with our project. The new subsidiary would determine if the project was appropriate for their business strategy. This was not good news because the subsidiary would have its plate full with little time to consider our project. We accepted the news as graciously as possible, considering that we were watching a $300,000 sale evaporate.

"We were at the point where the installation tapes had been cut, and we had done an awful lot of work leading up to it. We didn't react angrily to the decision because we really felt that we had a long term relationship with the bank, and we simply had to eat our costs. So we accepted their decision and went off to work with their subsidiary. They got busy with a lot of other things, and a year went by; and nothing happened. Later the bank told us that they had been prepared to offer us as much as $50,000 for the work we did on the front end.

"The next year the bank called to say that they decided to proceed with the project. The system that we had been marketing ran on IBM technology. They wanted the new system to run on a brand new technology that was taking the banking industry by storm for this particular type of application. The new technology had a unique computer architecture that basically, within reason, did not fail and ran all the time. It was uniquely appropriate for the application that the bank had in mind. At the time we hadn't done that system and had no experience with its application although we were very interested. We recognized its potential.

"What the bank wanted us to do was to develop a new version of our system to run on this new computer architecture. We were very interested in doing this, but we didn't have any expertise at the time. So we went to another company that later became our biggest competitor. They had substantial expertise with this architecture. We told them that the bank was going to issue a request for a proposal and asked them to work with us to revise our system for this architecture. They agreed to that, and we started several weeks of preparation in order to respond to the bank's bid.

"About a week before the proposal was due, we got a call from the other company -- our new partner and our soon to-be-competitor. They told us that they changed their mind and they were going to bid the bank proposal on their own. This put us in difficult circumstances.

"I recall my boss and I were on a business trip in Michigan, waiting in the Detroit airport and trying to decide what to do. Clearly we couldn't meet the specifications for the new architecture. That was the issue. We concluded that the only thing left to do was to call the bank. Just tell them what happened and say that we were sorry. We felt that it would have been difficult to have filled their requirements without a partner. So that day I called the president of the bank's subsidiary. I told him that I did not know what to say but that we were in a no-bid position. He asked if we could bid our old system. He said that would be OK.

"We went back to the office and packaged our standard proposal for the old system and submitted that against our competitor. The bid was awarded to us as the general contractor for the development of our system on the new architecture. In effect the bank was told us to go ahead and bid on this thing by ourselves, but we should understand what was being asked.

We were able to hire a very sharp systems design engineer who led the project so we were able to put the package together without a partner.

"The bottom line is that -- over the course of a couple of years and some trying circumstances -- my boss and I developed a pretty good trust relationship with the bank's Vice Chairman. When the subsidiary's president was confronted with the prospect of taking this significant capital decision to the Vice Chairman and the board, he wanted our name on the proposal because of their belief in our integrity. Getting us to bid the old product, gave them the opportunity to give us the business even though we could not provide what they wanted in our proposal. They believed that we would deliver the system that they really wanted, and subsequently we did.

"This episode sent us off in a new direction and that is interesting. It put us in software applications for this new architecture and made our erstwhile partner our number one competitor. Today, the system that was built for this bank represents some 80% of the technology that our business is built on. The seed money that flowed from the $300,000 engagement has resulted in an investment of tens of millions of dollars in that particular technology over the years. It drives about a third of all automated teller machines in the country and many of the regional networks. Our parent sold our division later and received 72 million for a business -- and eighty per cent of that was based on the technology that we developed for the bank.

"I look back and feel that we had an opportunity to deal with an individual of very high integrity who was willing to recognize that we were people with whom he could do business and wished to do business. His actions had a profound impact on the course of this organization. We might not have found another opportunity to get ourselves into the new technology and develop that product. We might never have funded it on our own. In those days, our parent was under a fair amount of performance pressure and didn't have money laying around to invest in R&D for a small division like ours. We really didn't have enough money to bankroll this thing on our own. It's really amazing how one single transaction had so much significance for us and would not have happened except for the Vice Chairman's integrity."

STUDY QUESTIONS

This is a story about the relationship between representatives of two companies -- those buying a service and those selling the service. The service, itself, is technologically complex and its outcome was uncertain. The first potential supplier did not have the competence, but the bank trusted their ability to get the competence and do the work successfully. The second potential supplier had the technological competence to provide the service, but had withdrawn its agreement to cooperate with the first supplier. The first supplier had done extensive up-front work without compensation. The bank was prepared to compensate the first supplier for this work, but the supplier did not ask to be compensated.

1. Was the bank obligated to compensate the first supplier for their work if they had been asked? Is this up-front work covered by the principle of avoiding harm?

2. Should the bank have given such weight to past relationships in its decision on the choice of the supplier? Should they have rejected the supplier whose proposal met their specifications for one that did not?

3. Was the bank's VP acting with integrity and avoiding harm to a supplier with whom they had a long term relation? On the other hand, was he irresponsible in handling the bank's resources?

4. Was the bank giving the first supplier what was justly theirs? Or were they being generous with this supplier?

5. Is there a place for generosity in business transactions? Or does this conflict with being the low cost provider?

6. The first supplier acted with integrity and honesty in its relation with the bank. Should this play a part in the Bank's decision?

7. Was the successful conclusion -- from the perspective of the first supplier -- attributable to their exemplary conduct?

8. Was it right for the second supplier to cancel their agreement with the first supplier and enter a competing bid? In this situation, did the second supplier have an obligation to avoid harm to the first supplier? Or is this acceptable conduct under the rules of competition?

JUSTICE AND HONESTY

A manager told me, "I was in the large equipment sector, and we bid large pieces of equipment for contracts worth anywhere from a quarter of a million, up to two or three million. These bids were to municipalities, governments, utilities, large industrial users and things like that.

"Often, we faced a dilemma on how much to tell potential customers, while protecting our interests. We build these large pieces of equipment; and, as you may imagine, we knew more about this equipment than the customers that were buying them. In some areas, we had more expertise than the vast majority of our competitors as well. In our industry, typically, customers would put specifications together. These, at times, would be a three- or four- inch book of drawings and specifications that would cover each and every part of the equipment."

"The manager, telling the story, said, "Oftentimes we'd look over the specifications, and we'd know what the customer had specified would not work. He had specified something that could be quoted at a lower price than a system that we knew would work.

"So now we are faced with three options. We can go back before the deadline for job quotes and attempt to argue with the customer and that can involve many people including consulting engineers. We would attempt to get the specifications changed.

"Or we can put in a quote that is an alternative to what they've asked with an explanation of why it will work better.

"Or, third -- and what we have done at times and what I've seen other people do -- we'd quote the system exactly as they ask for, and we'd put in a very low number so you know we'd get the quote. Then we'd go back and say -- after the contract is awarded -- 'You know, after we looked at this, and here is why it's not going to work, and we would have to change items one, two, and three, and that will cost another quarter of a million dollars."

I asked the storyteller, "Yes, so what did you do?"

He said, "Over the course of years, we have done all three. It is a situation where we would know, in any particular case, what competitors were bidding the job. Some competitors, we know, were much more prone than others to follow the third approach of bidding low on an unworkable system.

"So when we had a competitor like that -- and if we knew the consulting engineer for the customer was not an expert so the customer would be in the dark about what our competitor was doing -- then we would often follow the same approach."

I asked, "Do you think that was right?"

He said, "We tried to be fair when we made changes to the job after the contract was awarded. We knew that our equipment was better suited, many times, over our competitors' equipment for a particular job. In a sense, it was fair that we were giving the customer the best piece of equipment he could get. We were pricing it, even though some of the prices and some of the profitability of the job were made up after the quote -- after the job was finally awarded -- so the profit was made from the changes.

"Please understand that some of these changes are anticipated, but they are anticipated as things that are unknown at the time of the bid. When we went in, we knew we would be asking for these things, and we knew what we could charge for them after the bid. In some cases, we could charge just about anything because the customer really may have no choice. If we bid a three million dollar piece of equipment -- and if its going into a project with a two year build cycle and you're a year into it -- the customer has no choice. He can't go and put the project to bed for another year and wait for another piece of equipment like this. It's either take you to court and sue you after the fact or pay what you're asking for. We felt that the end product profitability with that job would provide an adequate return to all the stakeholders -- our employees, the communities where we work, the shareholders of the corporation. So we are providing a fair return to them and giving the customer the best piece of equipment.

"We are fair to the customer when we bid the system that wouldn't work because we'll make it work later. Now, of course, we're taking the position that we know better than the customer -- we know what is the best piece of equipment for them. In an open bid system, the whole object is for everybody to put their bid; and then the customer makes a decision based on the specifications, the bid prices, and the best equipment. So, in a sense, we're saying that we know better than the customer; we're going to do something that will get the contract; and, later, we'll show them the right way, being fair to all parties."

I asked the storyteller whether he sometimes followed the first option that he had mentioned: where he would explain to the customer why their specifications were wrong. "That way", I said, "the customer could act from more complete information."

The storyteller said, "Yes, we would go to the customer before the job was bid and explain why it wouldn't work and what we would have to do to make it work -- if we knew that we could work with the customer or consulting engineer (and sometimes both were involved) and if they respected our capabilities.

"The problem with that approach, though, is for some customers or consulting engineers are, in a way, unscrupulous. They would change the specifications and go back out to all of our competitors. The customer would say they had a system that really works, now bid on this. So we were teaching our competitors how to do the job right as well as giving the customer free advice that cost us. That's not fair.

"The fair thing is for the customer to come back to us and allow us to quote on an alternative piece of equipment without reopening the bidding. However, if it's a government bid or municipal bid, those people may not be in a position to negotiate a contract, but must reopen the bidding if they change the specifications. Then our only course is to bid on the unworkable system and negotiate changes after the contract is settled.

"Often a relationship of trust can be built between our company and the industrial customer and utility. Here we might work with them before the bidding or we might bid an alternative system, instead of bidding on their specifications. Of course, it depend on whether government funding was involved. With government funding, the industrial customer or utility might be required to take the lowest bid.

"Also, we have to be sensitive to the concerns of the customer's engineering people. These contracts have many steps for approval, and the engineers can look bad if we make an alternative proposal, taking exception to many of their specifications. When we work with an industrial customer or utility, we deal with one or two engineering people; but, when we bid, there's a number of financial people and other people in the upper management structure that would have to sign off. They would be suspicious of all the exceptions we took. It would make the engineering people look less capable. So we would attempt, before the fact, to change specifications."

I asked whether the strategy of being up front always worked. He said, "Sometimes, this strategy causes us to lose business. We would spend considerable time on the project's specifications and give the customer a bid with a number of technical details of the proper way to build a system. The customer would take that; and he would go and make changes to his specifications; and then give it out to other competitors. And often there were just two or three competitors. We spent a majority of time, compared to our competitors, analyzing those specifications and really getting to learn the system. Then the customer would set a rebidding deadline ahead a month -- for example from September 1 to October 1 -- and give everybody four weeks to submit a new bid. Our bid wouldn't change. And within the time window, often, our bid price would leak out to our competitors. So now our competitors know the system as we specified it, and they know our price so they now bid our system and come in below our price.

In this case, we know that the customer is going to leak our price and give competitors a longer time so they can bid our system. Then we use the approach I described earlier. We bid very low on the unworkable system and negotiate changes in the contract later."

I commented, "So you're saying that honesty is not always the best policy in business relations. Sometimes, you have to be less than open."

The storyteller said, "Yes, absolutely. Of course you can argue that we were truthful. We quoted on their specifications. Later we told them what it would cost to change their specifications. There was no falsehood. They did not ask us whether their system would work. That was up to their consulting engineer."

STUDY QUESTIONS

1. The manager telling the story cites three options: try to persuade the customer to change his specifications before the bidding takes place; quote on an alternative system than the one described in the specifications; quote on the unworkable system and negotiate changes after receiving the contract. Which option or options avoid harm to the customer and other affected parties?

2. The storyteller believes that they have been fair with all of their stakeholders including the customer when they used the third option. Do you agree? Explain your position.

3. What, if anything, is wrong with the customer using the information from the storyteller's company to revise the specifications and giving the competitors an opportunity to bid on the new specifications? Does this option avoid harm to the stakeholders? Is the customer being just?

4. What is the right way for the customer to respond to the storyteller's options?

5. Compare this story to "Justice and Generosity". Both stories deal with how customers treat work done

by a supplier before a contract is signed. What are the benefits and costs of the approaches used in each story? Does the customer have the obligation to avoid harm to the supplier in the stories? How does the customer undertake to avoid harm while representing the interests of its stockholders?

LIMITS TO AVOIDING HARM

The storyteller stopped to reflect between taking telephone calls, "Ethics has its limits in our industry. You avoid harming customers when they treat you fairly.

"We build off drawings when we get a job, and our drawings are supplied by our customer. Some of our customers are engineering firms who are designing facilities for their clients. We're given drawings by the engineering firms, and, then, we build tanks for their clients.

"The rule here is that -- if an engineering firm's client calls us and says: 'I have a tank that you built. Can you build me a duplicate?' Generally, we tell them, 'Yes, we have the drawings of the tank because your engineering firm had supplied them to us. But I can't go and duplicate their job because I would be working off their drawings. You should deal with the engineering firm.' Some people like to come to the fabricator and ask them if they can make a duplicate tank from the original drawings because they'll save the mark-up price of our customer, the engineering firm. So the client (end user) will try to go around the customer (engineering firm) and come right to us because we have the drawings, and we can build it right from that and save them some money.

"Generally we don't do that because it is not right, and we want to maintain good relations with our customers (engineering firms). Some fabricators do, however; and they get away with it.

"In some cases it's not unethical to harm a customer. We had a customer on the East Coast that 'burned' a lot of people including us. They went into Chapter 11 and 'burned' us for $50,000, and that is a lot of money for our company. Any amount of money is substantial, and I take it personally when people don't pay me.

"We're in a tough business where good margins are not easy to come by. If somebody would call us about a job originally engineered by that East Coast customer and ask us to do a duplicate tank, I would take a little different approach. I'd do the job to try to get some of the money back that the East Coast customer owed us. They are never going to pay us for the work that we did for them so this is a way to get some of the money. They didn't pay the bills that they should have paid, and most people would call them a bunch of thieves. Maybe this is at the borderline of ethics, but I feel that my allegiance to them or my duty to them is negated when I'm wronged -- and this happens to be financial. Other people may say, 'Oh no, you shouldn't really do that.' We would!

"Now I was talking about responsibility to our customers. Let me tell you about a client of the East Coast customer (engineering firm). The client had an explosion. I don't know if anyone was hurt or not, but it destroyed part of their facility. They called us to quote on building some pressure tanks. I walked in and talked to the fellow, and we had done work with them in the past -- similar type of job. They described the tanks to me that they wanted built.

"First off, they were showing us drawings done by the East Coast engineering firm. The East Coast firm had made the drawings and had a tank fabricator -- not us -- make the original tanks for the client. Now is that ethical for the client to do. -- asking us to use the drawings without the involvement of the East Coast firm? I don't know. But they did anyway, and they asked me if I wanted to quote on the tanks.

"I said, 'Number one, The East Coast firm is in Chapter 11.' Then I said, 'Are you aware that they are in Chapter 11?' He said, 'No, not really.' I told them that the East Coast firm has financial problems and all that sort of thing. I said, 'that was fine but that they want to keep that in mind.'"

The storyteller said to me, "As I told you, the East Coast firm had not paid us the $50,000 that they owe us. So when someone wrongs me -- and not paying my bill is one of the ways -- I feel that I have no allegiance to them. I am free to bad mouth them, and I did.

"Then I told the client of the East Coast firm that they were not the best people to have the tanks built. We certainly could build them and make them look very nice, and they would be better than the tanks they had -- and I am not patting myself on the back, just the facts. Anyone could look at the tanks and determine that.

"I told the client there was another tank fabricator in town that was financially sound, and they would probably build a better looking product at as good a price or less than the fabricator that had build the original tanks for the East Coast firm. So I gave them this other fabricator's name and number and that sort of thing. They talked with this other firm, and we did not get involved with the project.

"I could have said that we can build them and give the client a price and that sort of thing. But that comes under the heading of trying to do what's best for the client (the end user), you know. At the same time, I hoped that they would be satisfied with the tanks that they would get, and they would talk to us when other tanks come down the road. They'll feel that I was straight with them and forthright and give us the opportunity for future business."

I asked the storyteller why he suggested that the client go elsewhere rather than offering to build the tanks themselves. He said, "Well we could have built a tank that was better than what they could have obtained through the East Coast engineering firm, without a doubt; but it would have been more expensive because we have more expensive procedures and different processes. We could have produced the tank for them, but it wouldn't have been as economical. The fabricator for the East Coast engineering firm is what we call 'rot gut' shops. It is a term used in the field that means that they don't have approved procedures. They don't have certified welders; they pay bottom scale for their workers; and they use non-certified material. They just weld stuff together and ship it out the door.

"Well, things sometimes take an unexpected turn. I found out just this week that the client went back and gave the job to the same fabricator that built the original tank for the East Coast firm even though I suggested that they talk to somebody else. Probably, because of price. Also, their insurance company apparently wanted the tanks to be built by the same people that built them originally, and I don't know what the logic is behind that at all. Maybe, they saw it as replacing exactly what was damaged, not getting something better."

STUDY QUESTIONS

1. Do you agree with the storyteller's application of the virtue of avoiding harm to another? Why or why not?

2. The storyteller said that he turns down work where the client wants to avoid paying a fee to the engineering's firm. The client asked the storyteller's firm to make duplicate tanks from the drawing originally prepared by the engineering firm, but without involving this firm in the transaction. Is the storyteller being too scrupulous?

3. The drawings may be copyrighted by the engineering firm; or the copyright may become the property of the client when the original work is completed. Should that make a difference in the storyteller's decision? Explain.

4. The storyteller's firm was harmed by the loss of the $50,000. Does that justify his 'bad mouthing' the firm that went into Chapter 11 and steering business away from that firm? Does one avoid harming others whatever harm they have done? Are their limits to avoiding harm to another?

5. Compare this story to "Justice and Honesty". In that story, the storyteller felt that no harm is done if one is honest and forthright about the terms of the sale. In "Limits to Avoiding Harm", the storyteller turned away business because he felt the price/product combination was not in the interest of the buyer. He did not offer his higher quality/higher

price product and let the buyer decide. What approach is right?

6. Both "Justice and Honesty" and "Limits to Avoiding Harm" describe how they respond to customers who harm them. Compare the responses of both storytellers? Is one better than the other or are they applying the same principle to different situations?

BLOW THE WHISTLE?

"I was general counsel and also ran a division for a medium sized company. Our sales manager came to me for advice. The buyer for a customer had come to him and said, 'You're going to do a lot of business with me. I like to gamble a little bit so if you would see to it that I have $5000 deposited in some place where I'd have access in Las Vegas -- that would serve you well.'

"I said to the sales manager, 'If you want to take the guy to dinner -- you want to get him drunk, fine. You want to take him to a football game, terrific; you want to take him hunting, fine. I don't care if you take him hunting and spend $5000, but I'm not putting money into an account for him.' The sales manger said that we were going to lose business. I said, 'If we pay $5000, we lose more than the business. It's going to cost you $5000 more next year or $10,000 or $15,000. But mostly you have to live with yourself. That [expletive] is doing something he shouldn't do. He's hurting his company and he's hurting us.'

The general counsel told the sales manager, "It is not a question of whether we pay the $5000. The question is: are we going to blow the whistle on this guy. Now it's not your choice whether you can avoid getting hurt by this stinking business. It's your choice whether you blow the whistle on this guy. I hedged on that. I left it up to him and did not tell him what to do.

"About six months later, it came around another way. We were managing the tooling process for this buyer's company and bought tooling as directed by his company. We used this tooling in products that we made for this company. We bought some tooling from a Taiwanese toolmaker that they had set up to make their tooling. Some differences in the invoicing showed up that led us to believe that this same buyer was taking a kickback from the Taiwanese toolmaker. This was another five or ten grand. Well, these differences showed up in a

Stories of Virtue in Business

fashion that his company saw it, and they questioned us about it. They were reconciling all the costs involved. We really had no choice but to account for what we could, shrug our shoulders on what we couldn't account for, and hint at the possibility. Okay, ultimately, he got caught. He got fired. I don't know if he ever paid the money back"

I asked the general counsel, "You didn't directly blow the whistle? But you did not cover up the differences in the invoicing? Was this a punt?"

He said, "I wouldn't lie to our customer nor fake invoices. We didn't blow the whistle, but we gave them the information where they could draw their own conclusions. Two years later the buyer came back and asked us for a job."

I asked, "Didn't he have any idea how all this happened?"

The general counsel said, "He didn't think this was wrong. 'You've got five million dollars worth of business,' he reasoned, 'what the hell's five thousand dollars? I'm underpaid, he thinks. I'm in a position to help you. It is good for you; it's good for me; its good for your company. You're a great supplier, everything's fine for my company.' But my view is: Not quite! I'll tell you something, though. There isn't much of that going on. I would be very uncomfortable if it did."

STUDY QUESTIONS

1. The storyteller intentionally exaggerated what the sales manager could do short of depositing $5000 into an account for the buyer (e.g. "Take him to dinner"; "get him drunk" and so forth.). However it raises the question of where one draws the line. The storyteller in "Returning a Gift" thought anything of value was too much. The storyteller in "The Open Drawer" thought $500 was too much. In this story, the general counsel thought $5000 was unacceptable. The company in "Take the Cash and Run" was paid substantial sums to foreign officials. How does one draw the line? Explain.

2. The general counsel framed the issue as whether they should blow the whistle on the buyer by informing the customer of the buyer's request for a kickback; and he left it up to the sales manager to decide. The sales manager did not blow the whistle, but he did refuse to give a kickback. Whether he blows the whistle or not, he will do harm to himself and others. What harm should he avoid, and what harm should he accept? Explain.

3. The general counsel and his sales manager had a second opportunity to blow the whistle when they discovered that the buyer was receiving a kickback from a Taiwanese toolmaker. Again, they did not blow the whistle. Should they have? Appraise how they handled the situation.

4. The general counsel gives his interpretation in the last paragraph of why the buyer felt that he did nothing wrong. What, if anything, is exemplary in the buyer's conduct. What, if anything, is not exemplary?

PART III

ACTING HONESTLY IN BUSINESS RELATIONS

A quip by Mark Twain can be extended to honesty in business relations: Always tell the truth. It will please some people and amaze the rest. What he said was:, "Always do right. This will gratify some people and astonish the rest."[1] Acting honestly in business relations means that we provide the necessary information for others making sound judgments. The quip suggests that honesty in business relations is unexpected but admired. The managers who told stories about honesty thought it was exemplary -- out of the ordinary -- and that it was good business practice.

Honest executives are open and straight forward in their communication. They do not use information to manipulate the situation and mislead others to gain an advantage. The metaphor, perhaps, for transactions among honest business people is "garden"[2], while the metaphor for dishonest transactions is "jungle".[3]

Often, business is described as a jungle where winning is gained by force, stealth and politicking. I have never heard business described as a garden. The storytellers do not use the word, garden; but they do express the conviction that business is a place of integrity. They see themselves as honest with

---

[1] "To the Young Peoples Society, Greenpoint Presbyterian Church, Brooklyn [February 16, 1901], Bartlett, op. cit., p. 679b.

[2] Genesis 2:8-9. *The New Oxford Annotated Bible*, op. cit., p.3.

[3] Michael Maccoby. "The Corporate Climber Has to Find His Heart," *Harvard Business Review* (December, 1976).

each other, and they see their honesty having beneficial consequences.

The garden is seen as fun. It is productive and competitive, but one that relies on positive motivation, not force; on open communication, not stealth; on honesty, not politicking. The garden may seem to be a myth, but the storytellers believe they live in this garden. They use different metaphors to describe it as they tell their stories about honesty in business.

Seven stories about honesty are told in this section: "Never Lie"; "Professional Honesty"; "People Can Be Manipulated"; Graying the Truth"; "Honesty as an Executive Style"; "Take the Cash and Run"; and "Being Let Go". The storytellers believed that the interpretation and application of honesty is a major part of ethical practice in business. Indeed, the principle of honesty was applied not only in these stories, but in most of the stories.

NEVER LIE

"Never Lie" is an injunction given to the storyteller by his boss. It means, in the context of the story, that the storyteller should not deceive the company's customers. The storyteller describes his being offered a side payment and how he used this injunction to resolve that matter. He also tells how he uses this story and the injunction -- never lie -- in training his staff. The storyteller is committed to honesty as the way of doing business and attributes his success this mode of operation. He brought the principle of honesty to his business career and is glad that he found support by his colleagues and superiors in this mode.

PROFESSIONAL HONESTY

"Professional Honesty" describes an incident where an architectural firm acted without deception, and the storyteller attributes this to their professional code. The firm's act sacrificed its opportunity for business and increased the opportunity for the storyteller. The storyteller felt that it would have been easy to rationalize deception, and he admired the virtuous act of his former partners. Yet he was not surprised because this is how he acts. His markets are competitive, but he does not see them as a jungle. Professional honesty is nurtured in a garden.

PEOPLE FELT MANIPULATED

The story, "People Felt Manipulated", is ironic. The story-teller describes a superintendent and his successor -- he reported directly to both. The first superintendent gave and withheld information to deceive and manipulate subordinates, while the second was open and shared information and his own thinking. He describes his experience and feelings under both and concludes that he is a greater asset to the organization under the new superintendent -- that is he is more fulfilled in his work -- but he misses the operation's order and effectiveness under the old superintendent.

The storyteller is caught in conflicting values. He admires the honesty of the second superintendent and sees his own fulfillment in the environment created by this superintendent. Yet he sees the first superintendent's creative use of information as an effective management tool. He appreciates the order and rationality that the manipulation of information can provide an organization, and he is loath to give up this tool.

The storyteller does not resolve his value conflict in the story. Perhaps his career will be a journey that integrates virtue with the processes of management.

GRAYING THE TRUTH

"Graying the Truth" portrays a young president's struggle to know what actions are honest and to act courageously. For his organization's economic well being, he deceived some people who were good customers and good friends. At first, he rationalized what he was doing -- following his mentor's lead. Then, later, he agonized about what he has done and expresses deep sorrow. A similar situation occurred a short time later. This time he spoke honestly and courageously, and he now marvels how well the situation unfolded.

The storyteller found the rewards of business in the garden, not the jungle. He believes that virtue is good business. Even so, he sees himself committed to the garden whether more or less money is brought down to the bottom line.

HONESTY AS AN EXECUTIVE STYLE

In the story, the managers reflect on the Chairman's executive style. They describe how he infused honesty as a norm for the Company, and how this affected them. For these people, honesty means more than telling the truth when asked. It means open and full exchange of information among stakeholders. The Chairman's style was simple and straight-forward, but not one easily lived in business.

An unusual aspect of this story is the breadth of honesty. It is not only applied to a few stakeholders but to all -- customers, vendors, suppliers, and investors. In a sense, the Chairman no longer knows how to be dishonest. It is a life habit. Another unusual aspect is that the company operates in cut-throat competition with the industry characterized by thin margins. Yet the company operates as if it is a garden -- they would use another metaphor -- and they are highly successful.

TAKE CASH AND RUN?

The storyteller had the assignment of getting his company's money out of a Pacific Rim country that had exchange controls. The controls made it impossible to legally transfer the money out of the country, but bribery was an accepted practice for transferring the substantial sum in this account. The company's money had been accumulating in the country for over twenty years, and the controls were instituted after the company had made its investment in the country. The story is about the actions taken to transfer the currency out of the country, the bribes that were paid, and the losses that were suffered by the company. The storyteller dealt honestly with all parties but feared that he would be suspected of dishonesty and wrong doing and that his reputation would be destroyed.

BEING LET GO

A decision was made to let an employee go. This employee confronted the VP of operations on whether he was being fired. The VP felt that he had to give a direct, honest answer. The VP's boss felt that he should not because they needed the employee for a couple more weeks to complete a project.

NEVER LIE

"When my boss was explaining my position, he told me to abide by three rules: increase business; call him if I was getting into trouble; and never lie or deceive anyone. This was eleven years ago when I started with the company.

"This gentleman was then the director of marketing -- later he became the CEO. He was located at headquarters in California, and came to the Midwest to spend time with me. He reviewed my territory and various accounts and brought me up to speed on my duties and responsibilities. That is when he told me never to lie.

"I was happy to hear that because I wasn't sure what to expect in a sales environment. I was concerned about what I would be asked to do. It made me feel good to know that I would not have to compromise my integrity.

"Previously, I had been in an engineering-technical position; and I came to this company to take an engineering-sales position. I was apprehensive on what I was getting into. I had no formal training in sales, and I was a one-man operation to start up a regional activity for approximately twelve states in the Midwest.

"Interestingly enough -- two months after I started -- I went on a sales trip to the Chicago area to meet with a potential account. It was a situation where the account would be a re-seller of our services. In other words, he would make arrangements for his customers to use our software in connection with his computer services. He had a data center. He needed quality software to attract people to use their computers.

"In the course of the discussion about how the deal might be constructed, the gentleman asked me what my price was. I told him that we sell our services at list. He said that I didn't understand what he meant. I repeated what I had said, and he asked me whether I understood -- if I gave him a discount -- he would do a substantially bigger volume of business in my company's software relative to other re-sellers. I said that I understood that, but it would be an unfair advantage. He became quite frustrated and said that he would make me an offer that would be very attractive to me. He said we could do something under the table. He said nobody would know about it.

"It kind of caught me off guard. The account represented a large amount of potential business. Obviously, I had to make a decision and respond. What my boss had said was very clearly in my mind while the potential customer was talking, and I knew what was right. I knew that I should turn down the business for a good reason. And I did, and I never regretted it. Giving him a special deal would have required me to deceive my other accounts.

Our conversation closed in a friendly way. I think he understood that I wasn't going to deal contrary to company policy and compromise its integrity. He accepted it. Fortunately, nothing like that has happened since. It was so ironic that it happened when it did -- when I was young and new to this whole thing.

"My decision did not harm sales in the long run. That form of re-seller business diminished in our industry. There was a shake out, and there are only a few big guys left. So within four years, they disappeared. Of course, I did not know that at the time. Currently, I manage a staff of seven professionals in the region. Some come and go, but I continue to relate that story to them and tell them that those are my principles -- they are not to deceive people. If they do, they are gone.

"I did not tell my boss until three years later. He was in California, and I did not see him that often. Besides, I was hesitant and kind of embarrassed by the whole thing. Initially, I thought his reaction would be to ask me how I could be so stupid as to get involved with that or even walk into it. I thought that he would question my judgment on even setting up that call. Now -- sitting here eleven years later and having gone through many, many sales calls in all kinds of different situations -- I look back and realize that was an unusual event. I could not have expected to know what I was walking into.

"The opposite of deception is to be even handed. That is very important to us. This gentleman who was my boss and later CEO was always extremely careful to see that we treated our clients in an even handed way. Where situations occurred where one client or group of clients could get a better deal on our software than others -- he would never allow that to happen."

STUDY QUESTIONS

1. The storyteller believed strongly that he should never lie in his relations with customers. With Mark Twain, would you characterize his attitude as gratifying or astounding?

2. The storyteller believed that deception in business relations can not be hidden. Can it be hidden? Is it OK if customers don't find out?

3. The storyteller followed his boss' maxim with great success. Is honesty good business? What if the reseller portion of the industry had grown rather than diminished?

4. The storyteller trusted and respected his boss. Could he have practiced honesty with customers so easily if he had not trusted and respected him?

PROFESSIONAL HONESTY

"As you know, I'm an architect. I've been part of a professional group for a very long time. In this century, I think, honesty is the operating moral base that's valued. Giving credit is
one of the ethical things that I've observed architects doing.
This supports our working as teams. The architect employs
draftsmen, a structural engineer, an electrical engineer, a
whole group of people on a team. A project gets done by a
group of fifteen or twenty people. The architect is the one responsible and is the most visible, but he isn't likely to claim all
credit.

Somebody will say that 'so and so' did that building. Well
'so and so' didn't do that building, but that is the basis for selecting the architect to do the work. But an architect will be
careful to say what he or she did and to acknowledge who else
was involved. You can see it in an architectural magazine that
will show all the people involved in a building, who the team
members were and what their roles were.

"An episode happened about a year and a half ago that
shows the practice of honesty. I had left the firm where I had
been for twenty-three years, and I had started my own firm. A
piece of mail was delivered to my old company and addressed
to me. It was obviously something that they had to make a
judgment about whether it was for me or for them -- whether it
was intended for me as an individual or whether intended for
the company and directed to me as a representative of the
company.

"It was a big brown envelope with packing material, and it
had the return address of the Franklin Public Library very
prominently displayed on the front of the envelope. It was obvious from the exterior of the package that it was a request for
a proposal. Every architect in the world is looking for work. If
somebody had the opportunity to bid on the design, he or she
wouldn't pass on the request for a proposal.

"They could have called Franklin Library and asked them, 'Who do you want? David isn't here. What do you want us to do with your request for a proposal.' Of course, this opens the door to their responding to the request.

"It was first class mail. They decided that it should come to me unopened since it was addressed to me. In effect, they gave me the opportunity to do the job without touching the proposal. I think that was generous because they didn't have to do that at all. I might never have heard that the library was interested in a new building. As it turned out, I decided to decline. To me this is an example of honesty and integrity."

STUDY QUESTIONS:

1. Storyteller thinks that it would have been easy for his former firm to violate professional honesty & get away with it. He admires them for not taking advantage of the situation. Do you admire them for not keeping the proposal from the Franklin Library?

2. Why should the storyteller's old firm be honest, since they did not gain from transmitting the information to the storyteller?

3. The storyteller's old firm lost a business opportunity by sending the proposal to the storyteller. Do you count this as a loss to the firm? Should the firm still be honest or is it outweighed by the potential loss of revenue?

4. If honesty is just good business practice -- why be honest if there is no gain?

PEOPLE FELT MANIPULATED

"I'm not saying what it was that the last Superintendent did, but people perceived him as doing that. I've been in organizations where it has happened. I always thought that people dealt with one another openly and honestly. When they were patting some one on the back and saying, 'You're doing a great job and why don't you do a little bit more.' I thought that they were trying to help, but sometimes they meant something very different: 'You're screwing up here. Continue to screw up and you'll lose your job, and maybe I'll get more pay or more power.' I never saw that as an ethical question until recently, and I saw how people can be manipulated.

"I understand managers withholding information because I am a manager; but I think it is ethically correct to give as much information as possible so people can make the best decisions. My reason for seeing this as an ethical question was the negative situation during the last administration and the change with the new administration. A lot of people felt that they were manipulated. They were put into situations where they were supposed to accomplish something but not told what -- or they were told but no one else was. They were caught in hidden agendas that even they could not see; or they saw the agendas but couldn't talk to anyone about it. The former Superintendent would go behind closed doors, and confide in someone that he was going to take the organization in a new direction. The person would work in that direction; and, three months later, he was standing out there by himself -- that's when we cut the branch off.

"The former Superintendent was very authoritarian and very closed, but very effective. He was procedures oriented, and it was easy to follow his directions. You knew where he was going. He laid a path out months ahead of time. He was not liked because he was seen as manipulative. People felt that he used the situation, he used the people to obtain success for himself and his district. But that is not my opinion. I knew the Superintendent, and I did not think that was true.

"The new Superintendent came in, and decided that we should put together a mission statement or value statement for the school district. He got together a group of administrators, organized teachers, custodians, secretaries, food service workers, school board members, parents and some students. He had them sit down to write a value statement. Well, people were careful what they said, having just operated under this past Superintendent. The new Superintendent was trying to flatten the organization and open it up. He voiced this as a goal, but there wasn't a strong feeling that it would occur. Through all the meetings of groups and subgroups, there was a lot of ambiguity over who was setting direction. As these groups developed value statements, the new Superintendent added his comments and participated like everybody else, but he didn't take an active role other than doing that.

"Within one month, he was able to get the message across that there was a different leadership style, a different openness. He got people to see that they could come to his office and feel free to talk openly.

"Yet there is a negative side. Some people thought he had gone back on his word whenever he closes his door to make a decision. Some people waffled in making recommendations to him. Some tell him different things; and others pull in opposite directions. The only way to end the chaos is 'to close the door' and make a decision.

"For the most part, it has been positive. People feel that even when the decisions aren't their decisions -- they don't go in the direction that they wanted to go -- at least their voices were heard. Before people felt that they were muzzled, but some of the muzzling was self inflicted.

"Strangely enough, now that I've worked under both environments -- I can't say that one or the other works any better from the bench mark of practical operations. Even if we are not accomplishing more, we feel better about what we accomplish. In fact, I have the sense that we don't accomplish as much as we did under the past Superintendent. We no longer have the practical step-by-step method that we got from some one's marching orders. Many times we struggle though a project or make a presentation that doesn't go off without hitches. It used to go smoothly. It was clear what the past Superintendent wanted you to do. He was the focal point, and you could line up what you did with his expectations.

"The new Superintendent doesn't have a focal point -- it just floats around. It is difficult to make a presentation because you don't know if you are hitting his target. I guess I shouldn't concern myself with that, but it is difficult. There are great benefits in openness, but there are also weaknesses. Openness leads to a lack of clarity. Things are said that are inconsistent because they are not the final thought. When this happens in a public forum, the listeners feel there's a lack of leadership on the administration's part. Sometimes top administrators make presentations to the board and public that are in conflict with each other. It's not a battle, but different points of view and different information. I see this as a positive, but others don't. In the past, not everything was in line, but it was pretty close. The past Superintendent reviewed the presentations and had everyone in line. Openness is sacrificed for uniformity.

"The last Superintendent had an answer for everything. People didn't have to like it, but that's OK. It's the sort of leadership that people want at times. They may complain about his closeness, but they'd rather have a leader who 'calls the shots'. That way they can sit back and say, 'Well, that person made the wrong decision.' But when the actual leadership role is put back on them -- they find real difficulty with that.

"I thought I was losing a concrete Superintendent. I thought I would not survive in the new environment. In fact, I looked very hard for a different position during the first year after the new Superintendent came because I wasn't going to survive that type of environment. I had difficulties with it. It does bother me. My tolerance for ambiguity is not that high. I like things to run more smoothly even if information has to be withheld to accomplish it. But I found that I was able to contribute more to the new Superintendent than I was to the last. I bring something to the organization that he needs."

Stories of Virtue in Business

STUDY QUESTIONS:

1. Why was the operation of the organization more orderly and effective because of the former superintendent's deception?

2. The old superintendent sacrificed openness for the smooth running of the organization. Is it OK?

3. The storyteller felt more fulfilled in working for the open superintendent. Then why does he miss the order and effectiveness of the manipulative superintendent?

4. The storyteller said that he understood why managers withheld information -- he was a manager himself -- and presumably withheld information. Is it right to be less than open in sharing information if the organization is thereby more effective?

GRAYING THE TRUTH

"Two recent situations were a practical lesson for me on being up front with customers. These situations came together for I saw the second more clearly as a result of the first. Everybody sees somebody else's ethical dilemma as black and white, but you see gray when it's your own. Our company consults on marketing strategies and programs for consumer products and manages the implementation of these programs.

"We had worked with Company A for 17 years and took them from sales of 2 million to 125 million. It was a profitable account, making eighteen percent of our total revenue for the year. Last October, Company S bought our client, Company A. Company S had about 4 billion in sales.

"We were also consulting with "S", but on different matters than with "A". It was understood that our relationship with Company S was short term, and we were engaged on a project-to-project basis. The situation had been different with Company A. Here we were retained on an ongoing basis.

"One of our jobs for "S" was to assist them in locating acquisition candidates. Well one of their candidates was Company A; and lo and behold, they bought "A". We stepped back from what was happening and said that we may not be consulting with "A" much longer. "S" had depth in marketing expertise. They had an in-house marketing staff of at least thirty-five people. Our whole company has only fifteen people. So I saw for myself that our 17 year relationship was probably coming to an end. I started looking at the options out there and thinking, 'What will we do when "A" terminates our contract?'

"We're riding through November, December; and I'm starting to get some signals. The two family members that owned "A" happened to be best friends of mine. They were giving me signals that something was up. Well, lo and behold, on January 14, they terminated our contract -- giving us six months under the termination clause. So we were to be paid until July 1. They told us that the agreement was terminated so that we could work out a new one with their parent company, S. They were also saying that our agreement would have to be radically different than our past relationship. Instead of being marketers and executors of strategy, involved in the total business, we'd be more or less just involved in strategy. That means less income.

"Right away we started looking for other people to replace that income. Along came Company B, a half billion dollar company with no marketing expertise in Company A's products -- the business we built for "A". Company B wanted to enter this market because it was a natural extension of their product line and assets. So "B" wanted to put us under contract. Company B needed us -- and that would provide the basis for a long term relationship. On the other hand, any engagement with "S" would be short term.

"I had told Company B about the situation -- that we were under contract with "A" and would only be able to work with them after July 1. They said, 'it was OK to be under contract with A -- that was not a problem.' They wanted to retain us immediately, anyway. We could use the six months to get set up, and get ready to go, and to be ready to launch the program on July 1.

"We agreed -- more or less against my better judgment. I think greed probably overtook everything else. At first it was fine. March and April were great because all we were doing was sitting down and talking about packaging and concepts. Basically there was no disclosure of anything that would be a problem. Around May we started to pick out brokers and getting specific. The specifics were troublesome and started to look like a conflict of interest. We really backed off, and Company B didn't push too much. We just said, 'Let's wait until July 1 and then proceed'. "B" continued to pay us, and "A" was also paying us under our old contract with them.

"It was not a good situation. We were following the contract, no problem, according to the letter of the law. Even with regard to the spirit, we were not at all disclosing or competing. But it was unsettling to me because I did not want to have that appearance. In our business, appearances can be just about everything. I didn't feel comfortable telling people that we were working for Company B. I had never been in that position before. All the people that worked for me asked what they should do, what they can do, what they can't do. They were concerned because they had never been in that position either.

"Company A wanted to rewrite our contract, but we didn't want to do that. At this point, we told them that we wanted to work for a competitor (Company B), and that we were already working for them. Company A was not aware that we had been engaged by "B". Company A knew that "B" was in related products, but they didn't know that "B" wanted to enter their product line. Company A said that they didn't mind that we were working for a competitor in related products, and they still wanted to have a consulting contract with us. We went through the last three months of the termination period saying 'no' to "A". We said to "A" that we did not want to work with them after July 1.

"On June 15, Company A heard from some people that we were working with "B" on "A's" product category. The former owners of "A" still ran the company, and they called me and asked if we were working on this product with "B". I said 'yes'. I also told them that I had not competed with them and that we did not disclose anything. No matter what I said, they didn't believe it. Now our relation is a little bit better; time always heals these things. Its been two weeks, but they are still hurt, personally; also, maybe, professionally. The purchase by Company S is not final until a future date when "S" can exercise its option to buy; or if "S" doesn't feel its worth while, "A's" owners have to buy it back.

"I have lots of regrets. I learned from this situation, but my regret is that I didn't come right out and say, 'You know this is what they are asking, this is exactly what is going on.' I know that I would have slept better. I probably would have sacrificed fifty or sixty thousand dollars, but I would have been able to sleep a heck of a lot better. I would have just felt better. And not only myself, but my company would have felt better. This is not only affecting me, but it has affected our company in a negative way.

"My associate, who is my mentor, was actively involved. Company A was his account, while "B" is mine. I remember going to him at one point and saying, 'Let's just tell "A" the truth. What the heck? If we lose money, we lose money. We'll survive, and it is not that big a deal.' I said, 'Let's just tell them the truth.' He said, 'no.' If we had not taken on "B" at the time, we may have missed the opportunity. I went along with it. So it is my fault as much as anybody's.

"If we would have sacrificed the contract with "B", it would have meant forty-eight thousand dollars. So it wasn't that big a deal. We were having a very profitable year. Right now we are making more money than we ever made before. My esteem for my associate has been damaged because he doesn't need the money. We don't need the money. Company A could have made a stink about it; and they could have hurt our reputation. Now that I step back from it, I see that "A" could have hurt our reputation because we were not up front at first.

"It was one of those group-think type of things. On an individual basis, we were all for telling "A" about the potential deal with Company B. Then all fifteen of us sat down and talked about it; and, for some reason, we came to the conclusion that we should go ahead without telling "A". We rationalized it. Even though we followed our contract to the letter, it still was not right.

"On the flip side, our ethical choices were far clearer for the next opportunity that we got. Company A was a lesson that we put to work right away.

"We worked for a company that I'll call "C". We were with this company since its inception, seven years ago; and it was bought by Company "T" a few months ago. The owner of "C" had refused to let us work with any other snack food company, ever, even though he occupied a very narrow niche. He was always very competitive. As we feared in the case of Company "A", we figured our future with "C" was done when they were bought by "T". There was no way that Company T was going to retain us because they had plenty of in-house expertise. We had helped "C" position itself to be sold, and they did a really nice job and got a good price.

"When this happened, all of a sudden, we wanted to talk to a bunch of snack food manufacturers that had been wanting to talk to us. The thing is, you talk about a client being acquired but you never expect it to happen as quickly as it does some times. I made a call to a guy who's been bugging me for a year. Right away he's ready to sign a contract that pays us as much as we were making with Company "C" -- this was going on right in the middle of my "A" and "B" dilemmas.

"I told him [the company that wanted to sign the contract] that I was still under contract with Company "C", and I wasn't going to do anything unless I got approval to work with him from Company "T", ["C's" new owners]. We had a meeting on May 15 with "T's" people for the first time. I told them that they needed to tell me their short and long term objectives for us. I told them that I wanted to work with other snack food manufacturers who were not direct competitors. I said that "C" was a specialty chip company, and they won't let us work with other types of chips, breads, whatever. I said, 'You need to tell me right now what I can and can't do because I have these opportunities on the burner right now, people willing to work with me today. If we can't have a long term relationship, I'll work with you until the six-month termination is over, but I'm telling you, I'm going to be working for these other people. The June food convention is the big one for us, and I'm going to sign contracts with these people.' I said to them ["T's" people], 'This is it, on the table. This is what were doing. If you can't deal with it, tell me now.'

"So we discussed it. They didn't like 'this' and I didn't like 'that'. We went back and forth on which companies didn't compete with "C". We put it on the table and worked it out -- unlike what happened with Company A. I think that we gained respect from "T" because they found -- as we did -- that they don't have the expertise for "C's" niche but we do. We are going to have a long term contract with "T", plus we will have contracts with two other snack food companies that we agreed were non-competitive.

"I had the resignation letter ready for "T". I had it in my brief case with me. I was ready to pull it out and just say, 'OK, we've resigned, let's go through the termination period, and we're done.' And it worked out great.

"We learned that honesty's the best policy. It sounds simplistic, and it is amazing to me that it is so black and white. What happened was to the point. I fumbled on one; but the next, I handled with honesty and directness, and approached it in a way that was the best way. It happened the best way. Long ago your mom and dad told you that no matter what happens, no matter how big your problems, if you're honest, it's always going to turn out better. It takes a long time for you to understand that, and then it seems like you forget that when you get into business. At least I did. I was always very honest with our clients, and we never had that problem before. But it happened. I can rationalize it a lot: S is an outsider, it's a big company, they're not going to care what's going on. But rationalizations rarely help. What counts is what's on the inside in regard to your company; and how it affects your employees; and how it affects your clients. The way it affects your relationship with your wife, and things of that sort.

Your letter was on my desk for a long time. I felt that I didn't have any story to tell. And all of a sudden I realized I had something that, for me, was extremely important. I learned from my mistakes. That's the way I think of it. I teach people and allow them to make mistakes. I try not to allow myself to make mistakes. I'm very hard on myself when I make a mistake. I made a mistake here.

"In whatever business you're in, the financial downside it not always what you have to factor in. It is the very long term financial thing. I'm talking about the way the business runs internally. It's the way we trusted each other -- how our company and all our staff trusted each other. I think that the way we were approaching people the last couple of months tended to be more tentative. I think it hurt us -- and financially too. It's not a hard number. It 's a soft number in regard to what I lost. I lost at least a quarter of one million -- in productivity and in the interactions with our brokers because, all of a sudden, they knew there was something going on here that's not right. I think that it affected my working relationship with my associate and mentor. Right now I'm going through the process of buying the company from him, and I know for a fact that it is going to affect the way we do business with each other. We're going to be a little more cautious. The attorneys will get a heck of a lot more involved dotting the 'i's' and crossing the 't's'. I don't have the level of trust anymore, and that is not good. I think you should always trust the people you work with one hundred percent. I trust him ninety-five percent. But that five percent is not good. Your talking about millions of dollars in regard to buying the company.

"This episode will leave a scar that I'll carry for a long time. I know that for a fact. Also the people that work for me will be carrying around these things. I talked to my employees about it. We had a meeting in early June where I just told everybody my feelings about what we did. I told them that I did it wrong and that we're not going to do something like this again. I told them, 'If I do, kick me, throw things at me, get me out of this place as quick as you can.' I'd rather make a heck of a lot less money and feel better about what we're doing because in the long run we are going to make more money. We all talked about how we felt, and I think that was good for the company. But still you can talk about it all you want -- it happened."

STUDY QUESTIONS

1 Was it all right for the storyteller's company to work for "B" in the same product category while under contract with "A"? Why or why not?

2. Was it enough that they disclosed to "S"("A's" new owner) that they were working for "B" without indicating that they were working with the same product category? Why or why not?

3 Did it make a difference that they did not disclose any proprietary information about "A" to "B"? Why or why not?

4. The storyteller felt that it was wrong not to fully disclose what he was doing even though he disclosed no propriety information? He even had trouble sleeping. Was he being too hard on himself? Did the storyteller's mentor have the more practical approach or was he leading the storyteller in the wrong direction? The storyteller said that they were following their contract to the letter. Is not that enough? Why or why not?

5. Why didn't Company "A" make a 'stink' about the lack of full disclosure? Would it have damaged the reputation of the storyteller's company?

6. What was the difference in the storyteller's approach to "T" than to "A" and "S"? The outcome of the approach to "T" was more successful -- they got a long-term contract plus the right to work with certain non-competing firms. Was the difference in his approach to "T" from the others ethically neutral or not? Why?

7. Do you agree with the storyteller that honesty is the best policy? Why or why not? Is it always going to turn out better if you're honest?

8. The storyteller attributes his attitudes about what is right to his family? Would you attribute your attitudes about exemplary conduct to your family?

9. Did the storyteller experiment with how much to tell? If so, was his conclusion on the right course of action affected by his experimentation? Could he have come to his conclusion without disclosing different amounts of information over the course of the story?

10. We all have doubts about how much to tell. What would be your doubts in this situation? What were the

costs of not being straight forward? What were the costs of being straight forward? Is experimentation part of the learning process for developing virtue?

11. The storyteller said that we tend to see other people's ethical dilemmas as black and white but our own as gray. Did you see the storyteller's dilemmas as black and white? Why would we tend to do that?

12. Does it take courage to tell the truth? Why or why not?

13. One can fear that the truth may harm one's interests, and one can fear the consequences if one's duplicity is uncovered. Do you think fear motivates honesty, or does honesty arise out of the desire to be virtuous?

14. Does satisfaction in being truthful play a part in our exemplary conduct? Is one more likely to be truthful when it yields better business?

15. Ethics does not always flow from the top down. Sometimes it flows from the bottom up. In this story it flowed from the junior partner and protégé to the senior partner and mentor. Did this make it difficult for the storyteller? How would you handle such a situation?

HONESTY AS AN EXECUTIVE STYLE[1]

Living the principle of honesty was an executive style -- a way of life-- for the Chairman. He had rebuilt the Company, bringing it back from the edge of bankruptcy forty years ago and reshaping it as strong and profitable. The Company competes in an industry noted for its fierce price competition, and industry profits are thin. It makes large equipment to the specifications of buyers, and prices are set by bidding. The Chairman's guiding principle in rebuilding the business, he said, was honesty.

The story offers insight into an organization where the corporate leadership infused honesty as a guiding principle. The entire management team was interviewed to gain insight into his executive style.

One manager said, "I was in his office one day, and we had received a purchase order from a fellow who was -- to use the Chairman's word -- a crook. He told me a story about this fellow and then asked me if I knew why he was telling me this story. Then he asked me if I thought I could do business with a crook? 'Yes sir, but I think I would have to be very careful. Maybe cash in advance, whatever. But yes, I can.' The Chairman responded, 'There aren't enough hours in a day or night to watch a crook. If he is out to get you, he is going to do it eventually so you can not do business with a crook.' You know, the more I thought about it, the more I realized he was right."

Another said, "What has always struck me about the Chairman is that he is honest. He calls it the way it is. I can't give you any stories other than it's just something you know when you work for someone a long time. You don't lie to him. It doesn't work when confronted with his frankness." Still an-other manager observed, "I've seen people in the shop ap-

---

[1]This story is about the same person as "ESOP".

proach him on almost anything. It could be about part short-
ages or machine breakdowns or whatever. If you've got something to hide, you might have some fear talking to him; but
I've always felt being honest with him is the way to conduct
yourself. Even if something goes sour or the cost might exceed
what you originally thought, I've found that just talking with
him and explaining the situation -- he might not like it, but
he'll accept it."

"Anyone from a sweeper on up can come and talk to
him," commented a manager, "and they do. They can discuss
anything. A person, joining the Company, soon learns that an
open door policy is normal for us. It's just the way we operate.
Most of the officers operate this way because of the example
set by the Chairman.

"One thing too, we are not a large company -- 350 employees. You can afford to know 350 people. It's not uncommon for most people in the office at least to recognize most
people in the shop, and the reverse is also true. The Chairman,
at least once a week, walks through the shops, stops and talks
with employees and listens to them. There are social occasions
in which shop and office people get together. The Chairman
conducts large meetings of employees. There are a fair number
of questions about our financial condition, but we've always
been candid. Corporate-wide, there is no inhibition for people
to ask questions. By the Chairman's example, no one is put
down at these meetings; no one feels they should not ask questions or offer comments. Comments are accepted; but not always agreed with or acted upon. The Chairman is involved
with all these things and continues to use them as a conduit for
the flow of information and ideas."

This communication is based on the strong belief in the
truth. A manager reflected on an apocryphal story about the
Chairman. The manager said, "One story was about some sort
of court case involving the Company. For some reason or
other, the Vice President of Engineering, was to take the witness stand the following day. He appeared nervous about taking the stand so the Chairman told him, 'you are going to know
more about the engineering phase of the case than anybody in
the courtroom. Just relax, tell the truth and don't worry about a

thing!' The next day in the courtroom, the opposing counsel asked the Vice President if he had talked to the Chairman about the case before taking the stand. The Vice President said that he had. The lawyer said, 'Aha, what did the Chairman tell you to say?' the Vice President said, 'Tell the truth.' The opposing counsel was so taken aback that he said, 'No further questions.' It caused the judge and the people in the courtroom to laugh at the lawyer's discomfort. I'd say the story made an impression upon me; it probably made an impression on a lot of people."

One manager said emphatically, "If something goes sour for you, you just lay your cards on the table and tell the Chairman what happened. There is no way in the world I would lie. This is something I learned a long time ago in my career: you don't lie to cover up because eventually somehow it's going to turn around and catch up with you."

Another said, "Speaking your mind [forthrightly and honestly] is water under the bridge once the decision is made. It is not held against you; nor held for your benefit. You've voiced your opinion; you had your day in court. You don't revisit an issue 45 times. Life goes on." A third described the chairman as very supportive of managers' decisions: "I put my ducks in a row; provide information of what I feel is the situation; why it's not working out; and what I think ought to be done. Based on that, the Chairman asks me very good questions, but the bottom line is my judgment. It's more a final review of my decision to make sure that everything has been considered."

A manager reflected, "Tell the truth in handling complaints in the field. It means admitting that there is a problem with a certain item or thing. That can increase our liability tenfold in the future if word gets around that we have a problem. I tell them like it is. If we have a problem, we have a problem. We're bound and determined to fix it; we will work with them to get it resolved. We'll accept whatever responsibility for the problem that we feel is fair. That sometimes hard to do because we know what the risks are. Fixing a thousand compressors, for example, can be a rather expensive ordeal."

A financial manager said, "We have never felt that we had to be 'imaginative' or creative in our financial reports. We are very fortunate that no one has ever asked, suggested or hinted that anything should be done that was not on the up and up. If there is the slightest question, then we take the most conservative route. That has been corporate policy since I've been here."

An accounting manager said emphatically, "I won't tolerate anything that looks devious or underhanded. And it's never happened that my superiors have asked me to back-off. They have never said that I've been out of bounds or that they don't agree with the positions that I've taken. I started as a junior accountant and worked my way through the Company so I know what it takes to get the job done at various levels. As I've risen to my present position, my adhering to what is right - my ethical behavior - has never been questioned by any of my superiors."

"When I was hired," another manager related, "the Chairman and another officer sat me down and asked me questions, not just at one meeting but at several. They were very curious about my honesty. Not curious but emphatic that [honesty] was expected of every employee. I don't consider myself stupid, and I figured that we don't do anything improper at the Company."

Integrity in communication extends to gifts in the Chairman's eyes. His attitude is to accept nothing so nothing can interfere with one's judgment. A manager said, "a pen or pencil is an OK thing if it is nothing special. He will agonize over a package of cheese and generally rejects it."

An apocryphal story was used in orienting staff. In this story, the Chairman got wind of an attempt to shift volume from one period to another by getting shippers to issue shipping papers without having shipped the material. The Chairman said that was a "no no". the manager said, "When costs comes up, they come up; and that's it."

Another episode is about the Chairman's strong stand against product misrepresentation. One of the managers was told that some competitors at times sold used equipment or partially used equipment as new. He [the Chairman] is adamant that anything we sell as new is, in fact, new. He so strongly held this position that he confronted a competitor's president and asked him whether he was representing equipment as new when it wasn't. This person denied that his company was selling used equipment as new, but he was not very convincing."

The Chairman acts to insure that all parties in the Company's transactions are truthful. In one episode a manager was found to be embezzling funds. The Chairman insisted that this person be taken to court, and he was found guilty. A manager commented about the story, "What impressed me most was that the Chairman was personally involved. Cost wasn't an object in prosecuting this individual. The Chairman saw it through to a successful conclusion." The message sent through the Company was that this behavior would not be tolerated.

Fair exchange, as defined by contract, is the Chairman's norm. This means that the Company honors its agreements and expects its suppliers to do likewise. In one story, a distributor did not live up to a 100% of their bargain so the Chairman held back money. "It didn't go to court, but it got kind of nasty at times." The manager said approvingly, "He was right! If I spend a dollar, I expect to get the value out of it."

STUDY QUESTIONS:

1. Honesty for the Chairman meant more than responding truthfully to a specific question. It meant open communication with a full exchange of information. It meant respect and fairness in the communication process. What does it take to practice this kind of honesty day-in and day-out? Do you take the view that honesty requires the open exchange of information and mutual respect?

2. Honesty was the Company's guiding principle for more than four decades -- with each other, employees, customers, suppliers, and other shareholders. The industry is mature, and competition is based on price. Product cannot be differentiated. Deception is commonplace and accepted as the right thing to do in the

industry. Is the practice of honesty practical under these circumstance?

3. One of the managers expressed concern that telling customers about a problem with the equipment would increase warranty costs. Does honesty raise costs?

4. The Chairman is a charismatic figure and has been pivotal in creating a culture of honest exchange For the Chairman, honesty was its own reward, and he would conduct himself honestly whatever the gain or loss. Can this be expected of managers who succeed him as chairman?

TAKE THE CASH AND RUN?

"In the mid-60's, I was treasurer of a huge conglomerate, we'll call Worldwide Industries.[1] I had several financial functions reporting to me including internal audit. Now, that department often reports to boards of directors, usually their audit committees; but that wasn't the custom then.

"Worldwide Industries had a subsidiary, we'll call Superpumps. The subsidiary had a patent monopoly on certain equipment useful in many countries. Superpumps leased the equipment to distributors around the world who, in turn, leased the equipment to contractors. Distributors sent their rental payments to a Superpumps' bank account in their countries. The banks would hold the money in interest-bearing accounts, sometimes invest it in safe bonds, or send it where directed by Superpumps.

"During World War II, rental payments continued to be made to bank accounts in occupied countries, but the banks couldn't transfer the money out. When peace came, Superpumps transferred the money to its accounts in the United States.

"A Pacific Rim country, however, presented a special situation where we were unable to take our money out of the country. In 1942, Japan occupied it. After the Japanese surrendered, the country's leader proclaimed the nation independent of the former colonial power and named himself president. The United States supported this Pacific Rim country's proclamation of independence and put pressure on the colonial power to withdraw. Immediately after winning its independence, the country imposed foreign exchange controls so we were unable to transfer our funds from the bank in this country to the U.S. Nonetheless, the distributors in this Pacific Rim

---

[1]Names in the story are fictitious.

Acting Honestly in Business Relations

country continued to deposit rental payments into our account. Their culture fostered a strong ethic of paying one's debts.

"So from 1942 to 1964, about 23 years, the money had piled up in Superpumps' account at a bank in the country's capital. About $300,000 rested there.

"My bosses gave me the assignment to get that money out. I explained that the only way to do it was through bribery. The country's norm was strict about paying debts, but it recognized 'bakeesh' (bribery) as normal business practice.

"My superiors asked how much it would cost. I told them, 'In that part of the world -- if you want to get $25,000 out, you'd pay about 20%, say $5,000. For $300,000, it might cost about $60,000.' I said, 'It might take a couple of weeks to get the arrangements made through a 'fixer'.' You had to use a fixer in most of Asia, Africa, and South America to get this kind of thing done.

"I then explained all this to Jack Gallagher -- the man I selected to go to the Pacific Rim country to meet the fixer. Gallagher was about thirty, single with an engaging way about him. With us for about a year, he had done very good work.

"Gallagher flew to the country's capital. He was supposed to telex or phone me at least once a week.

"After three weeks with no word from him, I was concerned. Worldwide had another subsidiary in a nearby country so I asked them if they could check on Jack. They sent a man who then called me to say that Gallagher was in a fancy suite in the best hotel, living it up.

"A message went to Gallagher ordering him to meet me at the Baur au Lac Hotel in Zurich by the end of the week. A telex came back saying that it was going well, and he would meet me on Sunday.

"Sunday morning I arrived in Zurich. I arranged for us to have dinner in my suite so that we could count the money in private.

"At dinner he was relaxed and affable, a change from his usual energetic personality. I asked him why he'd had a suite at the best hotel. He said, 'The fixer made me move to the hotel and suite.' The fixer urged him -- he said -- to impress the people with his importance by living opulently. I let it go by because it could have been true.

"I said that we'd meet in the suite in the morning, count the money, take it to the bank on the Bahnhofstrasse where Worldwide had an account, deposit it, and return to the U.S.

"The next day we counted the money. Only about $140,000 was there in the country's currency. The currency had an astronomical exchange rate to the dollar so it was easy to make a mistake even though Gallagher had carried only large denomination bills.

"Laboriously -- and with increasing anxiety -- I counted it three times. After hours of this work, it was still about $140,000 in their currency. I said to myself that there should be about $240,000 here if you deducted the $60,000 that had to be paid in bribes. That meant to me that Gallagher had removed an amount valued at $100,000.

"I confronted Gallagher. He said that it cost a lot more because there had been an insurrection against the country's president last year. It was believed that America was behind the insurrection so we had to pay more than the usual rate for these things.

"'You should have called me and got my OK to pay more,' I said. I then asked when he had come to Zurich. He said, 'Last Thursday.'

"'So on Friday, you went to the bank, opened a numbered account and now have about 400,000 Swiss francs in it.' (The exchange rate of Swiss francs to the dollar was about 4 to 1 at the time.)

"He didn't deny anything; but, in effect, he said he would deny it if he had to; and we could prove nothing.

"'Well, Jack, as of now, you're fired!' He laughed again and said that he had thought this out. He said, 'Do you realize that you will be fired too! Headquarters would assume that you were in on it with me.'

"The shock of that idea had not worn off when he suggested that I take an amount valued at about $50,000 for myself. 'They are going to fire you anyway, so you might as well get something out of it.'

"'No,' I said, 'I don't do business that way. I don't take bribes. I don't steal from the company.'

"'They're going to believe that you did.'

"'I'll take my chances,' I answered.

"I put the money back into the suitcase, carried it to the bank, sat through another tedious count, and deposited it in Worldwide's account.

"Flying back to New York was no fun. I worried all the way.

"When I arrived at headquarters, I reported what had happened. No one uttered a word of suspicion about me or indicated any skepticism about my role. They all trusted me because I had been with the these men about a dozen years and had established a reputation as a straight arrow.

"We discussed what to do about Jack Gallagher. We called in the company's attorney. To every one's chagrin, he advised us not to try to prosecute in any way. We didn't have any evidence that we could use. Also, where would we go to court? Jack hadn't broken any laws in the United States, or in Switzerland; only maybe in the Pacific Rim country; but they would laugh at us if we brought charges. Even if convicted, how could we get him there to serve time?

"Besides, we didn't want any publicity about bribes overseas. Although it wasn't illegal in America at that time to bribe overseas, nobody wanted to admit doing it. Bribing was viewed negatively in the United States.

"You asked me what lessons I learned from this experience. The most obvious lesson is that I should have been in Zurich on Thursday. It was stupid of me to be so trusting. I should have met him when he go off of the plane and taken the cash from him right there.

"Also, I should have sent someone I knew a lot better and a lot longer. That $100,000 in 1964 is about the same a $400,000 in 1994. That's a big temptation, particularly when it was so easy to steal.

"Maybe the most important lesson is that it paid me to have a reputation for honesty. My bosses never questioned that. I worked for them another ten years, receiving several large promotions, getting ever-increasing responsibilities. All that led to a successful career, one that let me retire in honest affluence. That may not have occurred if I'd joined in the spoils.

"On the other hand, Jack Gallagher may have been sitting on a Caribbean beach for the last thirty years. I like to think that he has been kicking himself every day for not taking all of it."

STUDY QUESTIONS

1. The storyteller said that he does not take bribes or steal from the company, but he participated in bribing foreign officials to take a large sum of money out of a Pacific Rim country? Is this position justifiable?

2. The Foreign Corrupt Practices Act had not been enacted, and no United States law was violated for an American Corporation to bribe foreign officials in their countries. Is such action, therefore, justifiable?

3. What weight do you give to the practices that the government of the Pacific Rim country considered acceptable?

4. Is it relevant that public opinion in the United States considered bribing foreign officials unfavorably?

5. Was the storyteller honest in his dealings with his corporate superiors and Gallagher and his indirect dealings with the foreign officials? Did he hide anything or was he open in his dealings? Would you say he was virtuous in his conduct?

6. The storyteller took a risk in bringing the bad news to his superiors that Gallagher had stolen a substantial part of the money. *Instead, should he have taken the money and run?* He feared that they might believe

that he was a party to the theft. In retrospect, he believes that his reputation as 'straight arrow' put him above suspicion. Was the storyteller just lucky or did his honesty save him?

BEING LET GO

The vice president of operations told me about his firing
an engineer: "We had a quality engineer who was put on pro-
bation because of performance problems. He didn't get any
better, and then he made a horrendous mistake in judgment.
That was the last straw. We decided to replace him.

"The quality engineer knew it was a major foul-up. He
called me at home. He said, 'I think that I'm going to be let go.'
And I said, 'This in not the place to discuss this. Come and see
me in my office tomorrow morning, and we'll discuss it. The
quality engineer's manager had stopped talking to him so he
knew the news was not good. The engineer said to me, 'I think
you guys have already made up your mind that you are going
to let me go, and I want to know whether that is true or not.'

"I said, 'Yes, it is. Quite honestly, if it had been our pref-
erence on timing, we would leave you in place. We don't have
a replacement at this point. You asked me a direct question,
and I don't want to dodge it. I have to give you a direct answer.
You are going to be let go. Your performance is such that we
can't justify it any longer. You made commitments for im-
proved performance, and you did not follow through. We don't
think that we can tolerate your performance any longer.

"My boss, who reported to the CEO, criticized me for this.
He said that I should have lied. He said that we could have
used this person for another couple of weeks. We had a program going on, and we didn't have anybody to replace him.
My boss said that I made a mistake in telling the truth."

I asked the VP of operations whether his boss did this privately or at a meeting. He said, "Privately, but he also told everybody else."

The VP of operations told his boss, "He asked me a direct
question, and I couldn't evade the question. I couldn't tell him,
'Well, we're still discussing it.' Because we weren't." The VP
explained to me, "The decision had been made. He asked me a
direct question, and he deserved -- as a human being -- to be

given an answer that had already been decided on. You owe it to your employees."

STUDY QUESTIONS

1. Compare the approach taken by the VP of operations with that of his boss. How would you balance the need for the engineer to know that he would be let go with the interests of the company to have his services for two more weeks?

2. The VP's boss said that the VP should have lied. Should he have lied? What is your reasoning?

3. Is telling the truth a matter of integrity?

PART IV

RESPECTING OTHERS

Emily Dickinson, an American poet, contrasted those that respect others and those that do not; and her poem, "I'm nobody!", laughs with us at the pretension of those who *lack* this virtue:

> I'm nobody! Who are you?
> Are You nobody too?...
> How dreary to be somebody!
> How public like a frog
> To tell your name the livelong day
> To an admiring bog. [1]

The people that Dickinson admires are the 'nobodies', and she contrasts them with the 'somebodies'. The nobodies put on no pretense, but accept themselves and others as they are -- as 'nobodies'. They are civil toward each other and regard others as significant. The 'somebody' in her poem are unable to respect others because they are 'frogs' croaking to an 'admiring bog'.

Respect is a quality that appeals both to common sense and the teachings of the world religions, and it is stressed by the philosophy underlying quality management. It is very much a part of modern management technique. None the less, it seems difficult for people to adopt as a way of life. St. Paul

---

[1] Emily Dickinson, *Poems by Emily Dickinson,* Ed Martha Dickinson Bianchi and Alfred Leete Hampson (Boston: Little Brown and Company, 1948), p.15.

in his letter to the Corinthians, [1] struggled to impress upon this local Church that the members have different "gifts", and they should recognize each other's gifts and respect each other.

Executives can have more difficulty than some others in living the virtue of respect. Generally, they have substantially more "perks" than others in their business; and it is easy for anybody to confuse "perks" with "gifts". Access to a company airplane, for example, can be taken as a sign of one's competencies ("gifts"). So the more perks one has, the more signs of competence one has. Perks can be taken to mean that the executive is "somebody", and they can become a yardstick of the executive's importance. However, respect rests on the presumptions that everyone is gifted in different ways and that the diversity of gifts is to be valued by the business or any community.

Part IV has five stories: "Executive Parking"; "Putting It Back Together"; "The Glass Ceiling"; "Perks"; and "Respect for Employees".

EXECUTIVE PARKING

"Executive Parking" is a straight forward story about how a senior executive showed his respect for his company's employees. Shortly after being hired, he chose to park in the employees lot instead of in the area designated for executive parking. The dollar costs and benefits of his act are inconsequential, but the symbolic value is great. Symbolically, he was putting himself on the same level as others in the organization.

---

[1] 1 Corinthians 12. *The New Oxford Annotated Bible*, op. cit., pp. 1391-1392.

PUTTING IT BACK TOGETHER

"Putting It Back Together" is also about respecting others, but it is a more complex story. It is about an organization that had 'deposed' its executive director and was at war with itself. Another executive director was appointed after a long search. What distinguished him was that he had no track record as a leader and was unknown.

The strife continued after his appointment with the different factions demanding his support for their positions. However, he did not take sides, but showed his respect for the staff; while expressing disapproval for their hostile actions toward each other. Over the course of a year, the new head brought the organization back together. He was able to heal the organization and return it to productive relations without the mass firing and 'blood letting' that so often typifies such situations. He consistently respected his associates without approving their negative conduct toward each other. His manner was not to dissemble and to respect people for what they are rather than what they were saying.

THE GLASS CEILING

This is a story about a woman who decided to pursue a business career 40 or 50 years ago and about the impact that her career had on giving opportunities to other women. She started with a law degree which was uncommon for a woman at that time, was hired by a trust company, and eventually became its chief executive. The story is told from the perspectives of other managers, some who watched her assume leadership positions and others whose careers were directly affected by her success. She felt pressure to succeed because she knew her success or failure would affect the opportunities of other women. Her respect for others was a major force in efforts to break ground for others.

PERKS

The storyteller's judgment was that it was wrong for the CEO to continue to use expensive perks when employees were in the midst of a drastic cost reduction program. He felt that it showed a lack of respect for the employees. He could not work in this situation, and he resigned.

RESPECT FOR EMPLOYEES

The storyteller, the CFO, is strongly committed to the principle that everyone contributes value and is to be respected. In the story, she tells how she puts this into practice and why she is committed to working for her company. The story contrasts with two other stories in the book, "Perks" and "ESOP".

EXECUTIVE PARKING

"I was told where Mr. Johnson parked his car. He recently joined our company as a senior executive, and it might have happened on his first day on the job -- certainly the first week. I heard the story from more than one person so I assume that it was generally talked about in the organization.

"Parking can be a problem at our facilities that include the Company's headquarters and our largest plant. There is one massive surface lot for everyone with no assigned spaces except for the top executives who have covered spaces next to the building with their names on them. Everybody else has to hunt for a space. An individual can end up parking far from the building, having to walk some distance whatever the weather is, and that sort of thing.

"Well, Mr. Johnson parked in the surface lot wherever there was a spot instead of his assigned covered space. In fact he asked to have his name removed from the assigned spot. Everybody seemed to understand what he was doing. He felt that it was not appropriate for him to be treated differently from others -- to have special privileges because he was a senior officer.

"None of the other officers followed his example. They figured what he did was his choice. They didn't seem to resent it or challenge him. The organization is very hierarchical in its structure and, especially, in its culture. Privilege is a part of rank. At the same time, the Company has some strong willed individuals, and this is also part of the culture. Mr. Johnson did not lose stature because he did not exercise his privilege -- rather it was viewed at the top as an idiosyncrasy on his part.

"What struck me about his action was that here was an individual who had high personal standards, and he would adhere to those standards and not the social expectations that went along with his position. His position makes him highly visible in the organization, and walking a good distance from his car to the building drew a lot of attention.

"His action could have been taken as a commentary on the organization, but I don't think he meant it that way. Rather it reflected his view of people. He didn't see himself as distant from others or above people but on the same footing. I felt that he genuinely respected the employees and put himself at eye level with others. I did not see him as a 'revolutionary' in my dealings with him but as a strong willed individual who lived his principles."

STUDY QUESTIONS

1. What are some of the 'perks' in American business besides designated parking?

2. What 'statement' did the storyteller think the senior vice president was making by declining to use designated parking? Do you agree with the storyteller on the meaning of the senior executive's action? Why or why not?

2. Does the distribution of perks imply that some are more deserving of respect than others? Why have designated parking if some are not more deserving than others? What are other bases for designated parking? Handicapped? Visitor? Senior executive?

3. Can there be an equality of respect among employees with the unequal distribution of perks? Why or why not?

4. Are perks inherent in a hierarchal organization? Why or why not?

5. How do perks relate to productivity and continuous improvement?

6. An executive told the author that his company eliminated all designated spots for executives when

they moved to their new facility. Executives had to park in the general lot with everyone else. He said the employees did not seem favorably or unfavorably impressed. There was no comment. It just went unnoticed, he thought. Would you have noticed the change?

PUTTING IT BACK TOGETHER

"I was a health care provider, a youngster, relatively naive about business and business politics. In a flurry of changes that left some people scrambling, I was asked to look after administrative matters. I took the job on the assurance that there would be no political dimension to the work. The executive director, who made the promise, couldn't deliver because he was losing his grip on his own position. He had a series of health problems. He had become a day-to-day guy with little thought for the future of the organization. He was not very lucid at times. There were times when people would question his judgment and challenge him, and he was unable to mount an effective defense for himself.

"The power base in most health care institutions resides in physicians. Most of them were either unaware or didn't care about the management situation until it became obvious that systems were failing, and no one was looking ahead to the next move. The board split on whether to fire the executive director, and half of the directors resigned -- the half that wanted him out. Then the medical staff put together a memorandum saying that it would be in the best interests of the institution for the executive director to leave.

"I had left the medical staff and signed on as an executive just a month before the executive director left. Now I was asked to sign the medical staff's memorandum as their token representative. I did. I believed it, but it was not the right thing to do politically. My action did not cost me my job as it might have. There remained so few managers that the board could ill afford to see me go.

"The executive director's removal fractured the organization. Finance and marketing were very devoted to him and began acting defensively. This created barriers -- physical as well as gut feeling -- between them and the delivery system -- physicians, nurses and others who'd instigated the change. For about a year there was a very amorphous management with no one really in charge. The board sought an experienced director and were having difficulty agreeing on some one. Eventually they hired the fellow who's currently in that position. He inherited groups that were still angry at each other. They were pretty dysfunctional and hadn't communicated over the year.

"The lesson for me was how this fellow put the pieces back together. He articulated a mission that rose above the objectives of the warring groups and focused on the consumer of our services. He brought people back to a common objective.

"He led the transition from the staff not talking to one another, being suspicious of one another, to a situation where the staff was open and communicated with trust. He forced them to be together in one room and confront issues, not people. The staff considered themselves experts in each other's backyards and freely criticized each other. We went from an organization that was bent on making the other half look bad and punishing them to being a productive, cooperative and synergistic organization.

"Ultimately, the doors were open and it became possible to have the marketing person tell me, a finance guy, how to set rates; and the finance guy tell the operations guy how much money to spend -- without producing additional stress. In retrospect it seems like a phenomenal transition. That synergy has been an on-going thing for almost a decade now. It is difficult to think how dysfunctional we had been and how hard it was to work with the disparate elements of the organization.

"Putting the organization back together again, as he did, was all but impossible; but he did it. He built this team from warring elements. That must contain an ethical dimension. There must be something right in this town. There must be something right in the horse sense that results in a team staying together for the past ten years. He was even handed, instinctively fair, in dealing with the contentious factions; and he was compassionate.

"The executive director managed the components -- medical, financial, marketing and operations -- to diffuse power. One particular technique was very helpful. He steered criticism one step behind a manager no matter how clearly the problem lay at that person's doorstep. The message was

straight forward -- the manager or his function was off base --
but it was done so that the message didn't leave scars and bad
feeling. Another interesting technique was for the executive
director to get mad at the whole room when people start point-
ing fingers around the table and avoiding eye contact. It redis-
tributed the blame evenly. Rather than have every one leave
the table feeling exonerated and blaming others, they left
wondering what role they played in the problem. Also he focused discussion on what we could learn from the experience
so we could find a handle to deal with it more effectively next
time.

"He had a personal warmth so essential for a senior manager. He established a personal relationship that made people
feel trusted even before they demonstrated their abilities. You
could talk not just about business but about the personal implications of business -- for example, the family consequences of
long hours or the medical complications of work.

"It didn't go smoothly, especially at first. Most everybody's immediate reaction was to take offense at the idea of
distributing the blame evenly. They came to the meeting to assign blame to others and to absolve themselves of responsibility. They were looking for his support in identifying others as
being the source of the problem. He would have no part of
that. He would not spend a lot of time or energy back-tracing
every one's alibis and every one's blame-distributing behavior.
He distributed blame to everyone as gently and even handed as
possible and got us to search our souls for what part we
played, and he did this without disrupting work relations or
confidence about our ability to take action next time. There
was no need to fear when the heavy hammer would fall again."

STUDY QUESTIONS

The executive director's conduct showed an equality
of respect for his staff. By being Emily Dickinson's
'nobody', he changed his staff from 'frogs' to
'nobodies'. (see the introduction to Part IV.)

1. What is the virtue in refusing to assign blame?

2. Was the executive director's approach simply a ploy to effect change in the organization? Or was his style exemplary?

3. What is the difference -- if any -- between virtue and good management practice?

4. What might have been the cost of not going with the flow of malevolent action in this organization?

5. What risks did the executive director take in approaching his staff in the way he did?

GLASS CEILING[1]

Margaret McGinnis[2] who was the CEO of the Trust Company was a role model for women. She broke through the glass ceiling, and she sought to encourage others to do the same. As CEO, Margaret portrayed a style for women in business. She had seen the injustice in what opportunities were available to women in a publicly held corporation. Her mentor had been blocked by the glass ceiling that existed in the bank at that time. The mentor never became an officer of the bank even though she was doing the work of an officer and was recognized for her outstanding performance. In that era, it would not have occurred to management to make a woman an officer. Margaret ushered in a new era for the bank as she was promoted and eventually elected chief executive -- breaking the barrier for herself and other women that followed.

A protégé of Margaret mused, "From my vantage point, I guess, as I look at Margaret's outstanding career, not only her position as chairman of the Trust Company, but also her very respected board seats, there really was no position that was out of her reach. I joined the Trust Company in the late 70's when women were still fairly new in management. You still heard about glass ceilings; and here is a woman -- how many years ago? 30 years? 40 years ago? Broke all those ceilings wide open. She was a role model for people like myself and others that there really was no job not available to women."

The person, telling the story, said, "Margaret was ambitious, driven to prove herself, I think." Another manager said, "She did not give the impression that she was striving to show that a woman could be successful in business although she was competitive." I asked her about this and she said that she

---

[1] This story is about the same person as "Obligations to Clients" and "Standing for Autonomy".

[2] Fictitious name.

wanted to get the best job she could. Of course, over time, the 'best job' was a moving target; and eventually her goal became the job of chief executive. She also recalled a woman who had helped her and had been one of her mentors. The mentor had preceded her at another unit of the holding company by a generation. She had done an outstanding job; she performed the work of an officer; but she was never made an officer in her long career at the bank. Certainly Margaret must have seen this as an injustice arising out of a lack of respect for the mentor's abilities because she was a woman.

Margaret made a decision early to pursue a career in business; and, in that era, it was very unusual for a married woman to achieve that goal. As her career unfolded, she became conscious that her performance, good or bad, would change opportunities for younger women; and that increased the pressure on her to succeed. She had a deep respect for others and was committed to helping others succeed.

The storyteller, said, "Are you acquainted with ___ [a banking trade association]? It was, at that time, the premier banking association. It met a couple of times a year with outstanding speakers. Margaret was the first woman to ever appear before the group. I remember it well because there was some smirking about a woman being invited to appear before the group, and there was a great deal of curiosity about who she was. There were two or three well-known people, but she gave the best speech. I remember that because it not only gave her a great image, but it gave the bank some stature and standing."

Margaret said, "It wasn't that easy when I entered the national banking scene. I felt like a stranger. I recall entering a room, picking up a cup of coffee; but my hand was shaking, and I had to set it down." It was her first executive committee meeting of the American Bankers Association's Trust Division. Everyone else was a man, and her discomfort was only relieved when another member said, "Hello" and welcomed her in a most unaffected way.

A woman manager said, "I have to give the Trust Company credit under Margaret's leadership. I have to say, through out my career, I never felt held back for fear that a customer wouldn't accept me. Acceptance came earlier in personal trust, and later on the corporate side. But the Trust Company was always forthcoming in terms of allowing women to develop their skills and being willing to take a chance on both the corporate and personal side of the business."

The glass ceiling did not break easily, however. A long time colleague commented, "There were always people on these boards, who felt that no woman could run a business. A couple of directors said to me, 'Oh, she's a wonderful woman, but she shouldn't be president of the Trust Company.' They'd say, 'You need a good hardheaded man.' There was this attitude but it she did not show that she was bothered."

Margaret McGinnis projected a management style that was emulated by other women at the Trust Company. An officer, reflecting on her style, said, "She was already president of the Company when I started. Her fairness and judgment were respected by everyone who worked for her. She was a model for how to conduct myself as a business woman."

The officer continued, "Whatever they might have thought about a particular decision or a particular philosophy of hers, I never heard anyone say anything about her style that ever alluded to the fact that she was a woman, much less statements like: 'What can you expect from a woman.' or 'If she were a man, she would be doing this differently.' She was a very straight-forward, very honest, logical manager who knew why she was doing what she was doing, and communicated it.

"There was the question of whether a women president would favor women over men. The situation was quite the opposite in my view. She would not be easier on women than on men, and I think she made the women on her staff feel that they had to perform every bit as good as the men or slightly better to make the mark. I think some of the young women at one point felt that she was pretty demanding of them.

"I learned some lessons that some other women might not have learned because I was an officer under Margaret. There weren't many women in management positions then, and there was a strong movement to conform. For example, we were all expected to dress in navy blue suits with bow ties, and to imitate the way men were dressed. I observed that Margaret didn't do this -- she didn't try to be a 'man' at the office, dress like a man. She didn't even always wear suits which was the image some of us felt we had to follow. Or you weren't a businesswoman. However, Margaret wore dresses with jackets, professional clothes, and her mannerisms and dress were never designed to act like a man.

"Her approach -- and she was successful doing that -- encouraged me to resist the temptation to be like men to get ahead. And many women did give in and try to be like men to get ahead. I always appreciated this lesson. The best thing to do is remember that you're just a person doing a job in the organization, man or woman, and dress professionally and go about your business. She provided a valuable role model. No one ever forgot she was a woman and a lady. A lot of women felt more secure doing what everyone else was doing. Partly it's a question of attitude. Some people make an issue of conforming, and some people don't. Margaret McGinnis was just herself. She was breaking ground for other women at the Trust Company."

People at the Trust Company related that Margaret always advocated the aim of having more women and minorities in business without compromising standards. She encouraged women to continue their development in business. As an example, a woman officer related, "She hosts a luncheon every Christmas for working women that she encountered during the year; and it's a very interesting gathering. I've been invited for five years or so. Every Christmas, maybe a few weeks before, she hosts this luncheon. It's an interesting group of women who are there from all walks of life. A few years ago, Margaret had everyone stand up and talk about their past year and their hopes for the new year and sharing what's been going on in their lives."

"There was a different atmosphere here when she assumed the top position," as one manager saw it. "It was before business was aware of unfair treatment of women. So the impact of her becoming the CEO was significant to the whole organization. It brought home to us that we should judge people on their abilities. In that sense she had a great impact on the organization because, long before it became the thing to do, we did it. Later, we realized that this brought benefits because of the women's movement. But we cannot claim to have anticipated these benefits."

"Sex isn't as issue for me," a woman officer said, "I'd be kidding myself if I said it wasn't an issue earlier in my career. It was an issue. It was not as much an issue here as it would have been some where else. I can remember clearly my earlier experience with the glass ceiling: I had taken over a portfolio for a large company, and my department head -- who ended up being a good person to work with, a very big supporter of our efforts, and taught me a lot about this business -- well at the time he said to me, 'Gee, don't take this personally, but I don't know how the customer is going to react to having a woman. They have never had a woman manage their money before, especially a young one.' This was a business where experienced 45-55 year old males would manage corporate portfolios -- that was it. There were so few women in the investment management business, let alone young ones. As it turned out, the relationship went very well. But the question was raised and raised directly with me as well. 'Be aware. We're going to slot you but we don't know how the customer will react.

"I've had cases over my career of inappropriate things being said to me. I think it is worse to make an issue of it than to work through it. I have children; and, when I was pregnant, it was, 'Gee, what are customers going to say?' As it turned out, customers reacted very well. To this day, they'll say, 'how are the kids, and oh, I can't believe the boy is almost 12, where have the years gone?' It was a big issue behind the scenes though. Everyone was nervous. As it turned out, it wasn't a big deal. Margaret made great difference for this Company."

STUDY QUESTIONS

1. The CEO was a trailblazer in her company and industry to getting through the glass barrier. Her strategy was to dedicate herself to her work, perform ex-

ceptionally well, and aim at the next 'best job' from where she was situated in the organization. What differences existed in the strategy that she pursued from those that followed her? What strategy should a woman pursue today to reach the top job in a publicly held company? Do you agree with her strategy?

2. The CEO's respect for others showed itself in her view about her mentor. Could she have succeeded without the habit of respecting others?

3. How important was this virtue in her opening opportunities for other women?

4. What virtues should guide a person in their 'climbing the corporate ladder'?

PERKS

"This story hasn't as much to do with ethics as with management and being consistent," the storyteller said.

"I decided to leave the company. I was the vice president of production and reported to the chief executive (CEO). Initially, I thought I would wait and see how things would settle out. Quite honestly, we [senior management] were hoping that the CEO was going to bounce out, do something else, and we could manage the company the way that we thought it should. But it became evident after about six months that it didn't look like he was going to leave.

"I was not comfortable with the situation. It was clear to me that the situation was not going to change by itself, and I didn't have power to change it. So I needed to leave. That was the decision I came to. I wasn't necessarily accepting defeat. Initially, I thought that I could make this work. I realized that it was not me that failed or that I wasn't good enough to succeed here. It was the fact that I didn't have the power to change the situation.

"The situation was not right. I was either going to leave, or I was going to end up continuing to build internal frustration with the directions that the CEO was giving me. I took a 40% pay cut to return to my old job, and I gave up options that had tremendous potential.

"I was part of the new management that was taking the company from a family orientation to a professionally run company. The company was profitable, but there was opportunity to increase profits greatly by cutting the costs of purchasing and production. The previous management was making more money than they could spend, and they did not control costs.

"I was committed to cutting costs, but not the way that the CEO was going about it. I'll give you an example of what I found frustrating. I don't know if this is a matter of ethics or good management. You be the judge.

"We tightened controls on expenses and eliminated perks and the personal use of company resources. We said things were going to change and tried to set a different culture. The policy on company cars, for example, was tightened terrifically. Also, no longer could the maintenance department and everybody else perform personal errands for the executives. That was changed. I think that everybody would have accepted the new policies instead of complaining; but the CEO said, 'except for me'.

"The new CEO still lived by the old rules. He redid his office that had been redecorated recently by the previous CEO who had spared no expense. The new CEO just didn't like the style. So it was completely redone. We spent $100,000 just remodeling his office with a state-of-art sound system. He didn't have any problem with that.

"He had a company car for his personal use, and he also put his sister in a company car. The company subsidized his entire life style. He had a home that was about a two hour drive so the company was renting an apartment for him -- a luxurious apartment -- within easy driving distance of where we were. The company was buying his clothes and everything. It was subsidizing vacations. Some of this stuff was only known at the executive level, but some was obvious to everyone.

"All the while, the conditions in operations were tightening, tightening, and tightening. We had one series of layoffs because the market went down. We were going through a second cut, reengineering operations, and downsizing from a seven day schedule to a five day schedule. We told people that their historic Christmas bonuses were no longer forthcoming. We said that the company had to cut costs because it required higher performance standards. Employees saw what was going on at the front end [Executive Offices].

"The human resources person, who ended up leaving, told the CEO that we had a morale problem. He told the CEO that he [CEO] needed to go and talk to the people because they were having a hard time understanding the cutbacks. His response was an expletive. He said he didn't care what they thought."

I asked the storyteller what difference it made to him that the CEO didn't care what the employees thought. I told him that his job was going well. He said, "There is no respect, only contempt, when you don't apply the same rules. He showed his contempt for them and they responded in kind. He was applying different rules to himself as to them." He said, "People look to see if you're being consistent, if your actions are consistent with your words. That's very, very important. I think the first responsibility of management is to be fair. I resigned. I could not live in that situation."

I asked him whether his sense of integrity would block him from gaining a key position in business. He said, "If it does, it isn't worth it. Yes, I was blocked with that CEO. Without trying to overemphasize or over estimate my abilities, I think that I could have done anything this guy wanted if I had been willing to play the game. I think that I was more talented than the person that the CEO brought in as the executive vice president. The CEO wasn't comfortable with me knowing I wouldn't jump as high as he wanted me to. Therefore, I was going to be blocked. If I had dropped my standards, I could be making a lot more money than I'm making now and maybe eventually even run that company."

I asked him if a person of integrity can be trusted with power. He said, "Oh absolutely! More than a person without integrity.

"On the other hand, if your boss doesn't have integrity, they're not going to be comfortable with a person who does. The HR [human resources] person was doing a great job but had a high ethical standard and, privately, couldn't come to grips with the CEO's directives. He left as I told you.

"To be given real power, you have to be willing to march to the drum of those in power. The CEO was not comfortable with anyone who had a high degree of integrity even though he could predict what they would do. You should be able to trust people with integrity because you know what they are going to do -- what they think is the right thing. But, if that is not consistent with what you want done, you're not going to put an honest person in that position.

"You can rise to a certain level depending upon circumstances, overall performance, and technical proficiencies. At some point in time, your access will be blocked if it's known that you have a higher standard that you will follow if there is a conflict between what the CEO wants and what is the right thing to do. This is only true where the person with the ultimate power is not honest. Where I work now, the CEO has the highest [ethical] standards . Access to power is not blocked."

STUDY QUESTIONS

1. Compare this story to "Executive Parking". Both stories are about executive perks. The protagonists in both stories felt that executive perks was inconsistent with their respect for people. Do you agree with their thinking? What is your rationale?

2. In "Executive Parking", the protagonist did not use a privilege that was attached to his position, but he ignored the use of privilege by other executives. In "Perks", the protagonist did not ignore the use of privilege by his CEO and resigned. What would you have done? Why?

3. In "Perks", the protagonist commented on whether access to executive power is blocked for someone with integrity? What is you thinking?

RESPECT FOR EMPLOYEES

The chief financial officer (CFO) said, "My own feeling is that every employee contributes something of value to the company, and it's management's responsibility to recognize what attributes of the employee can be of most value. Management must bring forward those attributes because -- if an employee is contributing at a high level and where he feels comfortable -- the relationship works for the employee and for the employer. My own personal feeling is that you, the manager, need to be able to recognize personal skills as well as intelligence in an employee in order to have the best match for the person with the job. I don't think that there is an employee who doesn't contribute something. It is a matter of degree and a matter of fitting the person to the job.

I asked the CFO how she applied this at her company. The CFO said, "Personally, I absolutely consider it a personal responsibility. One of the things that is important to me is to provide an opportunity for those people that want to work. For example, we have working mothers, and we have -- obviously -- working fathers. We have people that need a flexible schedule to be able to work. We provide that. We try to rearrange the workload and scheduling and so forth in order to help people manage their own personal lives. You come back to the concept that says: if the person has a well rounded life -- they're happy at work and happy at home -- then both the employee and the company are winners, and also the home life.

"This is also the company's policy. For example, we have an on-site day care center that allows mothers and fathers to have contact with their children during the day. We have flex hours -- I have three people on my staff who work less than forty hours, and they choose the days that they would like to work. Some of them work the first ten days of the month and not at all during the last half of the month -- whatever works into their schedule and allows them to be good performers here.

"I feel very strongly it is collectively our responsibility to make people the best performers that they can be, and the company tries to do this. That is one reason that I decided to work here and stay here. Also, this is an environment that I want for myself. The environment encourages mutual respect, not conflict. One thing that I know about myself is that I don't like conflict. I always step back from conflict to try to resolve it so I can operate effectively. If someone is torn between home and work or between the job and supervisor, their performance is reduced. So I was happy to join the company. I knew the company and its founder for five years before joining the company, having managed their auditing for a public accounting firm.

"The company's respect for the individual reflects the belief of the founder. He fosters an environment of respect. One of his recent actions was to initiate a scholarship program for employees' children and step children. He was looking for additional ways to share his wealth with employees and ensure their success and that of their families.

"He started the company 27 years ago, and the founder reinvested all the profits over the entire 27 year period. Consequently, he has significant wealth. Over the years he has shown his respect for the value of employees and a willingness to share his success with them. The first thing he did was to share ownership with the employees in the form of a stock ownership plan. As the company got larger and larger, those participants became wealthy in their own right; but, at the same time -- for new employees -- it became less significant because the company was so large that no one employee could be a major shareholder. So he hit upon the scholarship program as a way to reach those that could not benefit greatly by the stock ownership plan.

"The plan provides four year scholarships that are awarded to 15 students every year, and each provides $1500 per year. The students are chosen from employees' children and step children -- if you think of it as an extended family concept. There are no conditions attached, but they are

awarded competitively. An outside educational agency is retained to make the selections.

"He is contributing the funds from his own personal
wealth although he obviously could have established this as a
company program. My feeling is that he has always been very
conscious of his employees and recognized their personal
worth. I was personally quite moved by the fact that this man
chose to use his personal wealth to help other people grow.
The founder was providing the opportunity to his employees'
children to grow and develop and become successful in their
own right."

STUDY QUESTIONS

1. Compare this story with Perks. The CEO in
"Perks" lacks respect for employees, while the CEO
in "Respect for Employees" has great respect. It happens that both companies are very profitable. How do
you account for this?

2. The VP of operations quits in "Perks"; while the
CFO is committed to staying with her company in
"Respect for Employees". Did they make the right
decisions? Explain.

3. What are the similarities and differences in the
ownership given to employees in "Respect for
Employees" and in the story, "ESOP"?

4. One story attributes the transfer of ownership to respect for employees, while the other to compassion
for their plight if the company is sold. How are respect and compassion linked?

5. Do you agree with the CFO in "Respect for
Employees" that both the employee and the company
are winners if you treat employees with respect?
Does the CFO's actions show a long term commit-

ment that is necessary to describe her as a virtuous person?

6. Would the CFO quit her job if she were in the situation faced by the VP of production in "Perks"?

PART V

JUSTICE IN RELATIONS WITH STAKEHOLDERS

Cardinal Thomas Wolsey was the Lord Chancellor under King Henry VIII. In his speech to Cromwell, Wolsey regrets that he has not been a just man. By implication, any administrator or executive is advised to be just and not fear the consequences.

> Love thyself last: cherish those hearts that hate thee;
> Corruption wins not more than honesty.
> Still in thy right hand carry gentle peace,
> To silence envious tongues: be just, and fear not:
> Let all the ends thou aim'st at be thy country's
> Thy God's, and truth's; then if thou fall'st, O Cromwell,
> Thou fall'st a blessed martyr![1]

Part V is about treating stakeholders fairly. Stakeholders include individuals and organizations that have a direct stake or claim on the value of the business. The claim may be specified by statutory and administrative law, economic bargaining power, cultural and religious values and moral suasion. Historically, stakeholders included stockholders, proprietors, creditors, unions and their members, other employees, vendors, competitors, and customers. Governmental bodies can be viewed as a direct stakeholder or as a force defining the rela-

---

[1]William Shakespeare. *King Henry VIII*, Act III, Scene 2, Line 441. Bartlett, op. cit., p. 211b.

tive claims of other stakeholders. The configuration of stake-holders is changing as a result of recent trends. Recent strategic thinking has placed greater emphasis on customers relative to other stakeholders. Also communities, women, minorities and environmental groups have come to be recognized as stakeholders.

In the context of exemplary conduct, **fairness** is the governing principle or virtue. It mediates and balances the exercise of law, bargaining power and so forth to achieve justice -- the ethically right claims of the stakeholders. What is ethically right -- within the theory of virtue -- is a matter of judgment and wisdom as tested by time. Virtuous executives are fair and fear not, as the quotation from Shakespeare suggests. What they do not fear are the negative consequences of being fair rather than 'politicking'. There can be a cost to just executives -- they can be "martyrs" to use Shakespeare's language. However, business generally believes that justice 'pays'.

Six stories had fairness as its central principle. These include: "Treating People Fairly"; Serving the Customer; Principled Action"; "Obligations to Clients"; "A Legal 'Bribe"; and "Jobs".

TREATING PEOPLE FAIRLY

"Treating People Fairly" was about a man who founded and 'grew' a bank. The storyteller, one of the bank's directors, said that the Board wanted to give this banker a very large bonus for the substantial increase in share price that was realized when the bank was sold. The banker felt, however, that some of this money should be set aside for employees who had contributed to the bank's success but would not be compensated through the sale of stock to the new owners. Some had not been able to acquire the bank's stock because their earnings or their length of service was insufficient. Others would lose their jobs under the consolidation, and they needed to be compensated for their investment of time in the organization. These stakeholders were among the least able to assert their rights, and they would have lost from the bank's sale. The

Board of Directors recognized the banker's position as fair and generous; and they set aside some of the gain to compensate these employees. Generosity is part of the cost of being fair.

SERVING THE CUSTOMER

"Serving the Customer' is about a man's recollections of his father. His father liquidated a company that he owned. The competitive situation required him to sell a product whose use, he believed, did not fit the needs of the ultimate user; and he would rather liquidate the company than sell an inappropriate product. His company was faced with a competitive situation where the buyers were not the user of the product. The buyers were contractors who bid low to get jobs so they needed to buy components at the lowest price. But the lower priced equipment lacked reliability, and the owner felt reliability was required for the ultimate user. The distribution system was a barrier to his communicating effectively with the ultimate user; and, in fact, the user might not even have been on the scene at the time the decision was made. The son said, "I did financial projections and showed my father that we could not make money the way we were doing business. We decided that we had better get out of the business before we 'went broke'. He liquidated the business rather than make a product that did not serve the user." The father was just and "did not fear".

The story has an ironic turn at the end. The son expresses skepticism that may be shared by some readers. He wondered whether his Dad would have made the same decision if he had not been well off. The son said that his father could have written a check for the whole thing without affecting his life style. He had seen many people acting differently, he said, when they got into financial trouble. The son concluded that integrity is expensive. Being fair to the customer called for sacrifice that everyone is not willing to make.

PRINCIPLED ACTION

A man recalled his grandfather's commitment to be fair in "Principled Action". The grandfather was well off but made sacrifices to do what he thought right. He placed himself in harm's way and was the focus of heated controversy, risking his fortune and his good name.

His grandson recalled stories that he heard about his grandfather when his grandfather was a young man. Even then his grandfather took positions against the main current. He wanted, for example, to reimburse a competitor when some of its supplies were accidentally taken by the company for which he worked. The president of his company stopped him from reimbursing the competitor, and this led eventually to breaking with the president. The grandson also recalled his own memories of his grandfather, and my impression from the stories is that he was a person of committed to being fair.

OBLIGATIONS TO CLIENTS

Margaret McGinnis was confronted with a choice where the right thing could cost her dearly and the wrong action would have little cost to her. A client of hers became gravely ill and was to have an operation from which she might not recover. The client had her assets in trust with the Trust Company, and Margaret was the trust officer for this account and knew the client well. The client had not signed her will so the estate might be distributed in a manner contrary to her wishes. Margaret made the judgment that the client was capable of signing her will even though hospital staff said she was confused. Margaret witnessed the client's signing the will, and faced a court challenge by potential heirs that threatened her reputation and livelihood. Margaret could have been a "martyr" except that her judgment won out.

A LEGAL BRIBE

Overland offered to buy the storyteller's company, and he also offered a package of benefits to the storyteller who was the CEO of his company. He would receive these benefits when the company was sold. The storyteller would lose the opportunity to remain CEO but he would gain the benefits. He rejected the opportunity of receiving these benefits, and he persuaded his board not to accept the offer. A couple of years later, another company made an offer that was accepted by the storyteller's board, but he received no benefits or compensation from the acquiring company as he would have from Overland. The storyteller saw the offer of benefits as a bribe and was prepared to forego the benefits and accept the loss of his job as CEO to do what he saw as right.

JOBS

An offer was made to the Board of Directors to buy their company for $23 a share. The negotiations extended into the meeting where the board was to make its decision. The board was in contact by phone with the acquiring company as it deliberated. The offer provided a substantial premium over the company's market value and was for cash.

The chief financial officer was a member of the Board and had to decide whether to vote to accept the offer. He was the last to vote, and the vote was 3-3 when the voting reached him. His boss, the chief executive officer, voted in favor of accepting the offer. The chief financial officer had given the matter much thought. He had even consulted with a member of a prestigious law firm on the legal ramifications of his vote. The price was satisfactory, but he was concerned about the impact of the sale on the employees and communities where the conglomerate had plants. He meet with the acquiring company and studied their financial statements. The acquiring company was highly leveraged, and he wondered whether their financial position might lead to a reorganization, and the reorganization would lead to the closing of his company's plants. The story concludes with how he voted.

TREATING PEOPLE FAIRLY

"Bill was president of a medium-sized bank when it was sold to a major regional bank. Bill's board of directors wished to give him a bonus because of his leadership in the growth of the bank and in the substantial increase in share price. The proposed bonus did not feel right to Bill. He told the directors that he would be well compensated through the sale of his stock; but many of the employees would not although they had contributed to the bank's success. Some employees had not been able to acquire a portfolio of stock because of their low level of income; while others had not been able to acquire stock because of their insufficient service; while still others would likely lose their jobs because of consolidation of their functions with the regional bank. These employees were part of the bank's success, treating them fairly required their getting a bonus at the sale of the bank. Long time employees, especially managers, would gain from the sale of their stock that they had obtained through the bank's stock purchase plan.

"Instead of compensating him, Bill proposed taking 10% of the proceeds and putting it into a pool for the employees. The directors realized that this was the fair and generous thing to do, and a fund was set up for bonuses for those not able to gain from the sale of their stock. He did receive a bonus -- somewhat lesser -- because of this, but he was willing to take money out of his pocket to pay the employees.

"The employees were, to a degree, overwhelmed. They knew that it was a very fair thing to do. There was allegiance to him. Some left when he left the bank. Four went with him to a new venture. Many others went to other institutions due to change in the corporate culture and the bank's restructuring under the regional bank. The employees admired him terrifically as a person and as a boss and manager.

"Bill applied his sense of fairness to himself. For instance, he did not wish his corporate position to be exaggerated. The directors suggested a very substantial amount of insurance on

Bill's life, in the neighborhood of three to five million dollars. He felt that the bank was not a one-man operation and this was not a good use of capital. Consequently, a lower amount was purchased. That year Bill had been president of a trade association and spent roughly half of his time away from the bank. He said that the bank was carrying on very well with a good team, and that he did not feel that he should be treated as privileged."

STUDY QUESTIONS:

1. Why did the president act so generously in recognizing others' contributions? What did he have to gain? Was it a matter of principle for him or were there economic benefits from his action?

2. Have you heard of other instances where fairness was the basis for recognizing claims of stakeholders?

3. How is fairness to be balanced with other bases such as bargaining power and legal rights for assessing claims by stakeholders?

4. Is fairness the norm in business for recognizing the contributions of stakeholders?

5. What parties have primary responsibility for making judgments about fairness? Chief executives? Boards of directors? Labor unions? Stockholders and proprietors? Governmental agencies? Employees themselves?

SERVING THE CUSTOMER

"Personal integrity was worth more to my dad than selling a product that was not right for those using it. Being fair to the customer was a matter of integrity. We had a business that manufactured emergency power generation equipment. It was intended to provide power for hospitals and other organizations whose need for uninterrupted power was critical; yet the equipment was sold in markets that were 'bid spec' -- high standards were not specified so these generators were sold as a commodity on the basis of price. The reason was that sales were made to general contractors rather than to users. The contractors were seeking to minimize their costs because they got their jobs by bidding low.

"So the market was saying to us, 'We want something cheaper.' Other firms came along who were willing to sell cheaper with, of course, these 'bidder specs'. I went to my dad and said that we had to have a line of 'cheap and dirty.' This is what the market place wanted. My dad said he would not put his name on that kind of product.

"His attitude was the death knell for our company because we lost market share. Up until the very end we continued to make a product that was designed to last far longer than our customers -- general contractors -- wanted. My father felt that the higher quality was necessary because the equipment might be needed in critical and unpredictable situations. He was building the best equipment he could, and he believed that his integrity was bound up in the performance of the equipment for unforeseen power failures.

"I did financial projections and showed my father that we could not make money the way we were doing business. We decided that we had better get out of business before we 'went broke.' He liquidated the business rather than make a product than did not serve the user.

"When we liquidated the company, we tried to find the people who owned our equipment. We wanted to let them know that we were going out of business. We offered to sell them spare part kits on components that were designed for our generators and could not be obtained elsewhere except at great cost.

"Out of the six or seven thousand generators we had manufactured, only five or six were no longer in service. The rest were operating and working. The feedback was very positive that I got from the people who maintained the equipment. They were happy because the generators worked and never gave them a day of trouble. This feedback from the field would have made my father proud. Some would tell me that our equipment was still working while their equipment from other companies had to be replaced several times.

"Our sales of spare part kits enabled us to liquidate the business by paying everybody. We paid the bank, and we paid our trade creditors. We found jobs for all our employees.

"One of the things I learned from this is that there are lots of ways to make money. Some are less than honest. Should we remain in situations where money can only be made by not serving the best interests of the customer [user]? Dad decided to get out of the business.

"Integrity and ethics are very expensive. That's something that you have to understand. I'm not sure what my dad's decisions might have been if he had not been able to afford what he did. They might have been different. Here was a guy who was able to walk away -- and he could afford to walk away and pay everybody off. Even if we hadn't run the spare parts business and made enough money to cover the liquidation, he could have just written a check for the whole thing without seriously denting his lifestyle. I've seen other people who got into trouble and who acted differently. I used to collect overdue accounts. I've seen people lose their integrity when they lost everything. I did collections for our family business for many years, and I've seen people do a lot of shady things. My father, however, had an iron will, and he was not going to backpedal."

STUDY QUESTIONS

1. What were the needs of the contractors who were his customers? What were the needs of the users who were the contractors' customers?

2. The owner liquidated his business rather than sell a product whose specifications did not fit the needs of users as he saw it. Was he being stiff necked in not responding to the needs of his customers (contractors)? Or was he being fair by representing a stakeholder -- the hospitals/users -- who were not 'at the table'? What are his obligations to customers and ultimate users?

3. Should he have relaxed his interpretation of what it means to be fair in light of the competitive circumstances?

4. The son asked whether integrity is only for those who can afford it. Do you agree with his implied conclusion that it is? Why or why not?

5. Many business men and women believe that their first responsibility is to serve the customer (contractor in this case). This means that you are honest in explaining what the product can and can not do, but ultimately you give customers what they want? Was the owner wrong in insisting that the customer buy what they did not want, rather than making what the customer wanted? Why or why not?

6. Does the owner's action conflict with the principle that the customer is king?

PRINCIPLED ACTION

Reflecting on the founder of the family business, the Vice President of Human Resources said, "All his life, my grandfather was a champion of personal freedom, individual responsibility and free market economics. He was a man who lived his life according to his beliefs and principles -- sometimes at peril to himself and his family. At times his reputation and business were at stake for he literally acted on what he believed. It wasn't just rhetoric; he put his money where his mouth was. He supported, with his own resources, the causes where his heart was. There was never any doubt that things would happen when Gramps got behind a cause.

"He was a great lover of people, all kinds of people. He believed in being fair. He had great tolerance for divergent viewpoints, but he knew what he was made out of. In as much as he accepted others, I don't think he deviated too far from his beliefs to please others. He had a wonderful sense of humor and a great, tremendous laugh. I still remember how he'd throw his head back and laugh from the heart. It was genuine. It was real.

"Gramps used to tell the story of how he never finished college. He was at the University of Wisconsin, I think, for a year or two. His father, whom I never really knew, asked him to leave school. I guess his father didn't have much time for higher education. He felt that his son ought to be out there doing something, not just studying.

"So he left school; and, at the insistence of his father, he was sent to an out-of-state foundry where the family had invested some money. I don't know that he had any interest in foundries then, but it was the first step in his eventually building a large, successful foundry business.

"Gramps was made the bookkeeper. As the story goes, he was there a year or two when an incident occurred that put him on a 'slippery slope'. A railroad train backed into the charge yard to deliver material that was not supposed to go to the foundry. Before he realized what was happening, somebody in the plant started to unload the freight car, thinking it was a normal delivery. When Gramps discovered what was going on, he tried to correct the error. Once you start unloading scrap metal, it very quickly becomes an indistinguishable pile, making it impossible to tell the new from the old.

"It was unrealistic to make an attempt to return exactly what was unloaded, but he wanted to rectify the situation. His idea was to send the balance of material in the freight car to the foundry that had ordered it and make restitution for the metal that was unloaded by mistake. When Gramps had his calculations done, he went to see the general manager and told him what he was going to do. The word came back that he was not to worry about it, and that he was not to say anything to anybody. The other company would not be the wiser.

"That attitude did not set well with my grandfather. It was the beginning of his desire to leave. It may not have been a big issue but it stuck with us as Gramps retold the story over the years. He did not do something immediately, spur of the moment. Yet he did not let it go and forget it -- continuing as if nothing had happened. In the railway car incident, he saw the firm's conduct not to be what it should be. He concluded that he wasn't going to tolerate continued unsatisfactory situations in the vain hope that they were going to get better. He felt he had to 'face the music' and recognize that he would be unable to change the company's attitude. The partnership was not going to be a good one. He could have spent the next six months trying to rationalize what happened. Maybe it was acceptable conduct because one of the railroad cars, destined for them in the future, would go to the wrong place; and it would all wash out and not be such a big deal. It is possible to rationalize anything away; but, when an ethical principle is violated, Gramps felt that one must correct it with all due haste."

All due haste was not long in coming. In a biography about Bill Grede it was reported that the general manager planned secretly to take control of the company from its investors.[1] "The general manager misjudged Gramps, and took him into his confidence, presuming that his loyalty had shifted from his family to the company. The general manager wanted Grede's help in pulling off the reorganization. At the general manager's request, Grede showed him how to get control without the other investors realizing it. Then he took a night train home and laid out the plan to his father. With this knowledge, the investors were able to force the general manager to buy them out, but Grede lost his job in the process.

"It was probably my grandfather's first opportunity to directly apply his idea of honesty and fairness in business. These were part of his belief in individual freedom and personal responsibility. They went hand in hand for him. Individual freedom for him implied personal responsibility to do what is right. It is one thing to speak of lofty goals, but another to live by them.

"We think about his principles of honesty and fairness and their place as key values of our company. We think that our foundries can't be successful if we don't treat everybody with the right amount of respect -- and that includes customers, employees, shareholders, suppliers and the community in general. Respect for our customers means delivering the product that we say we're going to deliver on time and at the price we agreed upon. We don't take orders that we have no intention of filling or cannot fill. We don't make promises without making our best effort to keep them. Of course, all businesses have operating contingencies that change production schedules, but we honestly try to do what we told our customers we would do.

"With suppliers, we recognize that they have to be profitable and that we shouldn't squeeze them, cheat them, or do anything dishonest and not in the spirit of fair play. For example, it is not ours to keep if a supplier sends us something and fails to invoice us. We don't suddenly get this windfall and not tell them.

---

[1]See Craig Miner, *Grede of Milwaukee*. (Wichita, Kansas: Watermark Press, 1989), pp. 30-33.

"As Vice President of Human Resources, I feel that we maintain an attitude of providing our employees fair wages for a fair day's work. We are certainly not looking to take something out of people or more from them than they are willing to give. In these times, people working in foundries just don't have the time or inclination to keep up with taxes, medical insurance and other benefit issues. I think that it is part of my job to make sure that they get everything that is coming to them. If someone, for example, overlooks applying for a benefit, I try to rectify the situation to make sure that each person gets what they deserve. Being honest encourages others to treat us with respect. Yes, Bill Grede, Gramps, left a lasting impression on our company, Grede Foundries."

STUDY QUESTIONS:

1. A freight car of scrap iron was partially unloaded when it was discovered that the shipment was intended for a competitor. Bill Grede worked out an arrangement for compensating the competitor, but he was told by the general manager that they would keep the shipment, say nothing and not compensate the competitor. Does fairness require that his company compensate the competitor? What is required in being fair to a competitor?

2. Mr. Grede's superior wanted to restructure the company to gain control. Mr. Grede put himself in harm's way by blowing the whistle on his superior and gave up a business opportunity. Was this a matter of fairness? Or was he being unreasonable in how the business game is played?

3. Mr. Grede had made up his mind to leave the company before this incident (restructuring the company). He decided to leave when he was ordered to be silent about the shipment that his company kept without compensating a competitor. However, he waited until

the incident to restructure the company before blowing the whistle. Would you have blown the whistle at the time of the first incident? Or would you also have waited? Why would you wait or not wait? (The first incident was when he was ordered to be silent about the shipment. The second was about restructuring the company.)

4. Knowing what is right doesn't always flow from the top down. Sometimes it flows from the bottom up. This creates a precarious situation for the subordinate whose integrity is at stake. What are alternative ways that one can handle a situation such as confronted Mr. Grede?

Obligations to Clients[1]

Margaret McGinnis[2] had to decide whether to put herself in harms way because of her obligations to her client. She did act to do what she saw as right even though the consequences could have been terrible for her. Many businesses say that their customers come first, but at what risk and what cost to themselves will they place their customers' interests first?

Margaret was president of the Trust Company, and she was also a trust officer and attorney, responsible for a number of accounts. One account was with an elderly woman, and the story is about her obligations to this elderly client.

A peer of the president related this story: "Margaret knew a woman well who was one of the Trust Company's customers. She became ill and was taken to the hospital with a brain tumor. The woman's attorney told Margaret that the elderly woman had not signed her will. The woman had procrastinated, and the attorney had been unable to bring the matter to conclusion. Now that the elderly woman was in the hospital with a brain tumor, the attorney was unwilling to take any further step except to inform Margaret of the situation. They both knew what the elderly woman's wishes were. The woman had told Margaret and the attorney that she wanted everything to go to her friend who had cared for her, and this is what the will stated. However, unless the will was signed, the estate would have gone to a relative very likely; and she had no contact with this person for at least a decade.

"Here she was in the hospital, and a will had been drafted but not signed. And now the woman's capacity to sign the will had to be considered. The nurses said she was confused, didn't know where she was, et cetera.

---

[1] This story is about the same person as "The Glass Ceiling" and "Standing for Autonomy".
[2] Fictitious name.

"Margaret came to me late one afternoon and explained the situation and said, 'I think we both should go to the hospital and see for ourselves because it would be a tragedy if she has the capacity and does not sign the will.' So we went to the hospital late in the afternoon. Margaret said, 'Let me speak to her alone for a few minutes and then I'll call you.'

"She saw the woman and came out and said, 'She knows exactly what she's doing et cetera. This was before the operation. So we went into the room; Margaret introduced me, and she asked her several questions. She answered them, and I could see she knew what she was doing. So the will was signed; and we witnessed it, knowing full well that there could be a challenge. That was before the operation. The woman went downhill very quickly after the operation and died. And, of course, the relative wanted the estate and challenged the will on the grounds that the court was being defrauded, making all kinds of accusations. The case went to the state supreme court where Margaret's actions were vindicated.

"Margaret was absolutely courageous about that. The easy thing to have said was 'too bad' and to avoid being accused of having done something that would have been a terrible thing for a lawyer to do. [Margaret was an attorney.] The elderly woman's attorney had not been a party to the signing of the will.

"It could have been an embarrassment for the Trust Company as well if the Court had ruled the other way. But Margaret's whole process had absolute integrity so there was no question in anybody's mind at the Company that she had done anything improper. It was clear to the people in the Company that her actions were absolutely legal and morally correct.

"I was very impressed by her action. The lesson for me was that we have obligations to people. It's a duty. Being in a position of responsibility requires us to do some things and be proactive sometimes. It was our logical duty to take steps to see that her wishes were realized. If the woman had not had the capacity to sign the will, there is no question in my mind that Margaret would have said, ' I'm sorry, she doesn't know what she is doing.'"

STUDY QUESTIONS

1. What Margaret McGinnis did was admirable but is it practical for every day behavior?

2. Do you think that business would support managers that took the risk Margaret took? These are risks to her reputation and the Trust Company's reputation.

3 What are the potential monetary costs of her actions?

4. What was the worst case scenario for Margaret and the Trust Company? The best case? It would appear that Margaret and the Company had little to gain in the best case scenario and much to lose in the worst case. If so, are her actions justified?

4. Could she have done this if she had not consistently met her obligations to stakeholders? In a sense she had no choice because she knew what was right and consistently had done what was right.

5. What if managers do not have the habit of doing the right thing for stakeholders. Could they have risen to the occasion as Margaret did in the story?

A LEGAL BRIBE

"For a long time, I had dreamed of being the chief executive of a publicly held company. The opportunity came to be CEO of Electronics[1] so I left my position as a senior executive of a multinational company for a job in the Midwest.

"The company had some problems. My first year saw heavy losses. The stock price dropped from $23 a share to $10.

"I divested unprofitable products, made some top management changes, and negotiated some beneficial acquisitions. Profits soared, and the stock rose from $10 to $50 a share

"Financial analysts wrote glowing reports -- the stock appeared on all 'buy' lists. Soon we were besieged with suitors who wanted to acquire the company.

"I wanted to remain as chief executive and retire from the company when I reached 65 -- in six years; and I wanted to keep the company independent. The board said that their first responsibility was to the shareholders so I must listen to the offers. I agreed that this was my first obligation.

"A spokesman for Overland Technologies, Inc. told me that he was sure he could convince Joe Deckum, their chairman and CEO, that Electronics was worth 1.4 times its market price and that was the highest multiple ever paid by Overland. That put the price at $70. I had no choice; I agreed to meet with Deckum.

"Having two bidders helps negotiations so I called another ardent wooer, Megamarkets, Inc. I said, "I think we're going to get an offer for Electronics at $70 a share. It isn't a firm offer yet, so you have a chance to go higher. Our minimum is $80.

"After some maneuvering back and forth, their CEO said they'd go to $75 a share on an exchange of stock deal, but no higher. I now had two bidders in play.

---

[1] Names in the story are fictitious.

"Joe Deckum of Overland invited me to meet him in his skyscraper office on the East Coast. I accepted.

"We sat down in his grand office with a magnificent view of the city and ocean. He said that he never paid more than 1.4 times current market price. The arithmetic hadn't changed. It was still $70.

"I told him that I had an offer at $75 on an exchange of stock basis. I explained that the transaction would be tax-free to our shareholders. The tax-free aspect, I said, was very important to some of our larger holders.

"He said his offer, at 70, was for cash, but he knew that much of our stock was held by pension funds and foundations, so the tax-free aspect wouldn't help them. Also, cash was a hard value, but the value of a stock deal could decline at some point.

"I said that I didn't think those were sufficient grounds to turn down a higher price.

"Then came the sweeteners. He said that -- if the deal went through on his terms -- I'd get a 20% increase in salary and a large batch of stock options in Overland stock.

"I would become vice chairman of Overland, with an office in the tower on the ocean side. He said, 'You're 59 so you'd retire at 65. That means that you would never be chairman or CEO, but you could work on acquisitions, or on community projects, or industrial associations, things like that -- whatever pleases you until you retire.'

"He took me to lunch at the United Club, one of the most prestigious private clubs in America. He showed me its beautiful rooms, decorated with expensive art, its many facilities. Then he said, "As vice chairman of Overland, you'd get into this club. We pay all fees, dues and expenses, of course.'

"He took me to a large room adjacent to the Library. Big scrapbooks covered a long conference table, and others were set on specifically built shelves along the walls. These scrapbooks contained pictures of meetings at an estate owned by the club. He said, 'the United Club sponsors and organizes get-togethers. As a member of the club, you'd get to go to their annual get-together.' The get-togethers lasts for three or four days and always includes many prominent people.

"I browsed through some of the scrapbooks. It was mostly pictures of famous people in a relaxed atmosphere. There were pictures of top-echelon business leaders and top leaders in politics and government, occasional foreign dignitaries, sometimes a prominent author -- all kinds were in the scrap book.

"It was 'good, old boy', networking in action. It was the most coveted networking session in the world. Some men would 'kill' to attend these conclaves.

"Joe Deckum could see that I was impressed. I felt that he was offering these sweeteners along with reasons to get me to persuade my board to accept the $70 cash offer.

"To me, it was bribery, but not illegal bribery! At that time, the regulations were vague as to how much of these personal inducements had to be disclosed to shareholders. I think that it still is not clear. Quite often -- after an acquisition is completed -- the acquired CEO is enriched by the acquirer, if he has been cooperative in the negotiations. He goes on the acquirer's board, gets an increase in salary and bonus. Many payments and benefits are possible. Sometimes he leaves shortly after the deal with a golden parachute far in excess of what he would have received from his own board

"I didn't come down from my $80 price, so the deal collapsed. Some might think I was foolish not to accept Overland's offer and end my career in such a prestigious situation.

"I then persuaded the board not to accept Megamarkets' offer of $75.

"Eighteen months later, we sold the company to a new suitor for $120 a share. I received nothing extra from the acquirer, but I did cash in my stock options, sold my stock, and retired. Nobody has to hold any benefits for me. I never got to the 'get-togethers' of the United Club."

STUDY QUESTIONS

1. Do you agree with the storyteller that the payments and benefits offered by Overland were a bribe although a legal one?

2. Could you consider the payments and benefits simply side payments for work performed or was it an inducement to do something wrong?

3. The storyteller lost his opportunity to remain as chief executive and retire at 65 from an independent company. Should he be compensated for this loss by benefits such as those offered by Overland? He was compensated by the increased value of his stock, but was that already his property?

4. He points out that it was not uncommon for CEO's to accept benefits in this type of situation. Should he hold himself to a stricter code than the general practice?

5. Did the storyteller do the right thing?

JOBS

"I have another story. Maybe this was not an ethical decision, but it was a tough one. Our company had a lot of takeover attempts that you read much about in the paper. In the late 80's, this fellow, Jack,[1] approached the company; and the negotiations were brought to the board. The board had seven members. There were five outside members and two inside directors including my boss (CEO), and me.

"Jack wanted to make us a very generous offer. I accompanied his people, visiting our plants; and our CEO and I were down to his office, overlooking the confluence of the Monongahela and Allegheny rivers. Jack was the type about which movies are made. Started out as a welder; young; very wealthy. He flew to our headquarters in a black helicopter.

"I never really trusted Jack. He was offering $20, $22 a share. I had some real concerns that his companies were flimflam. I was really concerned about our responsibility to the communities where we had plants; and I was concerned about the businesses in these communities, and about the people who worked in our plants.

"So I went out on my own nickel and retained an attorney on my own just to get some advice. I wanted to know -- in my responsibilities as a board member -- whether I should be concerned that the bidding company was so highly leveraged that our assets would be leveraged and lost. People would lose their jobs -- communities their businesses. The attorney told me that it was valid to consider the impact on the communities under state law, but the primary concern were the shareholders. So my advice from the law firm was -- yes, I could consider other stakeholders as well as stockholders.

"So we had the board meeting. The bidding company was on the phone, making the offer; and we got $22 a share; and

---

[1] Names are fictitious.

we started voting. We had discussed all the pros and cons. The CEO voted in favor of accepting the offer along with two outside directors. Three outside directors voted against accepting the offer. So the vote was 3-3 when it was my turn to vote -- I happened to be the last to vote. I voted against and that killed it. The deal fell apart. The stock drifted down to about $15. Fellow board members asked me how I could do that [vote against the offer].

"I don't know. I just had bad vibes about the guy. I had enough sense not to do anything wrong as a director. The attorney told me that I had every right to consider the effect on employees, on communities, in addition to the shareholders. The directors that wanted it to happen asked how I could turn this down if I represented the interests of the shareholders. My argument was, 'Well, that's true, but what about our employees in our plants? This guy is a flimflam operation. We just take $22 a share in cash and kiss all these communities good-by?' I didn't think that was right."

I asked the storyteller how the CEO reacted. "The storyteller said, "I had some reservations about being on the board. My boss (CEO) said, 'When you're a director, you vote as a director. We will maybe disagree.' But we didn't disagree often. He did exactly what he said. There were no repercussions whatsoever from my voting different from him.

Jack, the guy making that offer, turned out to be a crook. He had bilked five banks. Half of the companies he had were not incorporated. There was nothing. I just felt this guy didn't look right to me. I did what I thought I had to do. I voted no.

STUDY QUESTIONS

1. Should other stakeholders be considered beside stockholders in the decision to sell the company?

2. Did the storyteller strike the right balance among the stakeholders -- the communities, employees and stockholders?

3. Why did the storyteller seek an attorney's counsel before making his decision on whether to accept the offer?

4. How did the virtues of adhering to the law and compassion seem to enter into the storyteller's decision to reject the offer?

5. Compare how the storyteller resolved the issue of selling the firm with the stories: "Treating People Fairly" and "ESOP"?

PART VI

KEEPING PROMISES/COMMITMENTS

Keeping promises and commitments would seem to be conduct that is an ordinary standard for business transactions; yet the storytellers felt that such conduct was exemplary. Several stories were told where promise keeping was the major theme that characterized the action. Most stories, nevertheless, included promise keeping as a sub theme and part of the action while other virtues were being accented.

Promise keeping is a dominant theme in human history and is expressed even in the play of children ("Cross my heart and hope to die."). It has a central role in the Hebrew Scriptures where it is the story of the covenant or agreement between the Lord and the Hebrew people. Both 'sides' make promises of what they will do with regard to the other. The covenant story describes the interplay between the Lord and his People as the promises are carried out in the people's history. It shows the Lord's faithfulness to his promise along with his almost pulling back, at times, in the face of the people's intransigence. Many episodes are included of the people's backsliding on their promises to the Lord. The theme of promise keeping with its variations is played out during the course of the People's history. It shows the struggle of the Hebrew People to be faithful to their promise, falling short of their commitment and renewing their promise. Being true to the covenant is what matters most. The rainbow is the image that the Lord gave them as a reminder of the covenant:

> And the Lord said, 'This is a sign of the covenant
> which I make between me and you and every

> living creature...I set my bow in the cloud, and it
> shall be a sign of the covenant between me and
> the earth. When I bring clouds over the earth and
> the bow is seen in the clouds, I will remember
> my covenant which is between me and you and
> every living creature of all flesh; and the waters
> shall never again become a flood to destroy all
> flesh.'[1]

Breaking promises is a matter of betrayal and is seen as abhorrent within the human community, yet it also has been justified by the human community: "The public weal requires that men should betray, lie, and massacre."[2] Shakespeare portrays the tension between promise keeping and betrayal in his tragedies very powerfully.

Promises are matters of the utmost importance in capitalism and can be formalized in contracts. Sometimes, they can be enforced by the legal system under appropriate circumstances; but the law is a cumbersome and costly way to enforce commitments. Many commitments are honored or ignored depending on the ethical standards of the promise giver, and these are the situations described in the stories. The stories raise the question of where the obligation to a promise ends.

Six stories are included in this section: "Sticking to Our Promise"; "His Word Was Good"; "A Servant Leader: A Steadfast Tin Soldier"; "Accepting Responsibility"; "Standing for Autonomy" "What is a Commitment Worth?"

STICKING TO OUR PROMISE

"Sticking to Our Promise" begins with the storyteller recalling an episode that goes back to the founding of the company and that has been retold through generations of employ-

---

[1] Genesis 9:12-16. *The New Oxford Annotated Bible,* op. cit., p. 11.

[2] Michel De Montaigne. *Essays.* Book III, Chapter 1, "Of Profit and Honesty." Bartlett. op. cit., p. 99b.

ees. The story's moral was that the company would adhere to its promises, even at great sacrifice to themselves. The story-teller said, "This is an image that lives in our relationship with all of our stakeholders, even in the smallest matters. Doing what we say is a matter of integrity."

Then the storyteller related his recent experience when the purchasing department was added to his responsibilities. He took on these duties in the midst of a decision on changing vendors from one that was a major company to one that was small, and a substantial amount of money was involved. Their policy was to invite one bid and allow no re-bidding. The small company's bid was below its larger competitor. The larger company pressed for the opportunity to re-bid to cut its price much below its small competitor, and it offered plausible reasons for allowing a second bid.

The storyteller was inclined to permit re-bidding because of the savings for policy holders. The purchasing manager who reported to him insisted that they stick with the one-bid process because of the principle, "One bid, one shot. We don't play games." He went along with the purchasing manager's position although he thought "we were cutting off our nose to spite ourselves". The small firm won the bid, and now both vendors are striving to give the best service, and the storyteller sees lower costs down the road. He has come to believe in the principle of sticking to one's promise.

HIS WORD WAS GOOD

"His Word Was Good" is about a senior vice president who managed several of the company's affiliates. One was a "data affiliate" that provided software and information services for operations both within and without the company. Other affiliates that the senior vice president managed were "user affiliates", and they used the services of the data affiliate.

The company wanted to evaluate the performance of the data affiliate, and the senior vice president set up a team composed of user affiliates to do this. The team intended to compare the performance of the data affiliate against that of the competitors; and, to make this comparison, it needed to learn about the software that was offered by competitors of the data affiliate.

The competitors were reluctant to provide information for fear that this would give the user affiliate an advantage. The storyteller said that the senior vice president gave his word to the competitors that the information would not be given to their data affiliate and would remain confidential. The competitors were persuaded to cooperate.

The senior vice president and the team kept his word. They did gather the information and were able to compare the performance of the data affiliate with that of competitors. The user affiliates changed their information systems as a consequence, dividing their business between the user affiliates and its competitors.

The storyteller said that the senior vice president's action set an ethical framework for the user affiliates in dealing with the data affiliate, and the precedent made it easier for the user affiliates to do business with the data affiliate's competitors. The ethical framework provided a basis for determining when it was right to exchange information with the data affiliate and for dealing in an even handed way with the data affiliate and its competitors.

A SERVANT LEADER: THE STEADFAST TIN SOLDIER

"A Servant Leader: The Steadfast Tin Soldier" combines two titles. The steadfast tin soldier was the storyteller's characterization of the protagonist in reference to Ilyich Tchaikovsky's *Nutcracker*. I added servant leader to the title in reference to Isaiah 42. "He did not cry nor lift his voice or make it heard on the street..."[1]. I had known the protagonist professionally for many years, but I was not aware of his story -- his steadfast and self effacing support of a succession of a

---

[1] Isaiah 42:2. *The New Oxford Annotated Bible.* op. cit., p. 873.

college's presidents and his leadership in radically changing the college. His public posture was of an administrative assistant although his actual role was a combination of aide-de-camp and executive vice president.

The storyteller said, "He was the first male allowed in the 'inner sanctum' and he scared everybody. He was a big person, and just his walking through the hall sent shudders through the staff. He 'ruffled their robes.' The guy was so careful of every word and every mannerism so as not to draw attention to himself. He was courteous, gentle, sat with his hands down on his lap, never pushing his feet out and always deferring to the president. I think he'd made a promise to himself that he was there to serve the religious order of nuns and that this was to remain their institution. He was steadfast about never taking their power but being there to empower them to run their college in spite of changing times."

With the presidents, he led the college from one that was small, largely unknown in the region to the largest 'small college' in the region -- highly visible. Its vision and culture changed radically from being inward looking, serving a small community of students and teachers, to being visionary and outward looking into the region, serving a diversity of students and educational needs.

American management tends to be assertive -- jungle fighters -- while this individual's promise led him to be self effacing and gentle. The situation was unusual so the question is whether the virtues that he embodied have application in other situations. Could American management be gentle and self effacing and succeed? His conduct came from the heart, but could he have been just as successful by using a more assertive style of leadership?

ACCEPTING RESPONSIBILITY WHEN THINGS GO WRONG

"Accepting Responsibility When Things Go Wrong" describes a tragic episode that was widely reported in the press. However, the story -- told here -- is not about the events as such; but it is about an employee's reaction who heard reports of the events as they unfolded. She was not a participant in the events but an employee-observer giving her response to the tragic events and the reaction of the company.

The storyteller had committed herself to the change in culture being fostered by the new CEO. She said that she had gone through a lot of training to instill new values in the organization -- empowering people, accepting accountability for one's actions and working to one's full potential. This meant accepting failure as well as success and not shifting blame to others. The new CEO had promised his commitment to these values.

When the tragedy occurred, the CEO apologized publicly, and said that it was the company's fault. He took responsibility for the accident. Keeping his promise to be accountable strengthened the storyteller's belief in the company's culture. She said, "That really sent a message to the employees. First, we really felt bad about it. We all felt responsible in some way. This was a strong message on how to be accountable for something." The company kept its commitment.

STANDING FOR AUTONOMY

Margaret McGinnis was the chief executive of a trust company that was a subsidiary of a holding company. As the chief executive of the trust subsidiary, she faced the alternatives: on the one hand, she could oppose a change being considered by the holding company and resign if she lost; or, on the other, she could go along with the proposed change and keep her job.

The holding company had banking subsidiaries as well as the trust subsidiary, and the change would involve reorganizing trust operations from being a separate subsidiary of the holding company to being a division of a banking subsidiary of the holding company. This banking subsidiary was the holding company's flagship bank. Some of the nation's bank holding companies had trust operations organized as separate subsidiaries, and some had trust operations organized as divisions of banks so there were precedents for either form of organization.

Her predecessors as chief executives of the trust company had made a commitment to the principle that there should be a complete separation between trust and banking activities (a Chinese Wall) and that this was best supported by having banking and trust operations organized as separate subsidiaries. This view had been formulated as a consequence of discussion over many years and successive generations of executives and was an important aspect of the trust company's culture. Margaret had considered the issue carefully, and she was committed to the organization of trust operations as a separate subsidiary. She saw this arrangement as an important tradition and as critical for the success of trust operations. Consequently, Margaret stood for her commitment and risked her position as chief executive of the trust subsidiary. The story showed, other managers said, that it is sometimes necessary to stand for what you believe.

WHAT IS A COMMITMENT WORTH

The CEO and the VP of Operations decided that they wish to expand their warehouse space. The space is leased in a building that has sufficient unused space that is not under lease. They approached their landlord before their lease expired The landlord offered terms that he said were 'rock bottom', but they were not satisfactory to the CEO and VP.

They negotiated much better terms with a competitor of the landlord. After discussions among themselves, they agreed to go forward and made a 'handshake' commitment with the competitor. On hearing of what the company had done, the landlord offered terms that were more attractive than the competitor's. They turned down the offer because they felt that their honor was worth more than $100,000. The landlord came back with even better terms that was worth $200,000 more than the competitor's terms. The storyteller then tells how they responded to the landlord's offer and what his personal reaction was.

STICKING TO OUR PROMISE

"Adhering to what we promise is a core value of our Company," the Director of Administrative Services told me, "and this value marked the Company's first days. We were founded as a mutual life insurance company in 1859, and very shortly after that -- and I am going to guess that it was within two years -- there was a train wreck in Wisconsin. A cow stepped onto the tracks, and the train crashed. I was told that fourteen people died, and two were our policy holders. We had death claims to pay; but, as a brand new company, we did not have enough money collected to pay these claims. Our claims were $3500, and that was $1500 more than we had on hand. So the founder and the directors put their own money into the pot to cover the claims. This is an image that lives in our relationships with all our stakeholders, even in the smallest matters. Doing what we say is a matter of integrity.

"Recently, purchasing was added to my responsibilities; and I inherited a decision to change vendors. The Purchasing Manager, who reports to me, had decided to substitute a small vendor for a major vendor; but the decision had not been implemented. We have lots of equipment manufactured by the major vendor. Ironically -- and perhaps problematically -- the small vendor was offering to sell or lease the very same equipment as manufactured by the major vendor. We liked the major vendor's equipment, but they gave us a bid that was higher than the small vendor.

"Then the major vendor came back to the Purchasing Manager a number of times explaining that they had made the wrong bid. They gave about three or four reasons why -- they said -- they had not given us the right bid; and they wanted to resubmit it. If we had accepted their revised bid, we would have saved a substantial amount. In the short run it would have been a gain for our policy holders, but we felt that the bidding process was clear. We were certain about our directives to vendors that we had one-stage bidding, and we were confident that they knew of our being very, very consistent in this matter. Our one-bid process invites bids from suppliers; and the lowest bid, meeting our requirements, is accepted. Re-bidding is not considered. We don't play one bidder against the others and say, 'Guess what, we've got a lower bid -- can you match it or beat it?' One bid, one shot. We don't play games.

"Well, I thought we were 'cutting off our nose to spite our face after the major vendor came back with a better price. I really had to wrestle with that one. Well, again, we would have saved money in the short run; but, in the long term, we reaffirmed the integrity of our system that says one bid means one bid. We do what we promise.

"And, you know, I've come to learn that as soon as you allow one exception, you no longer have one bid. You have thrown the whole thing out the window, and I was very impressed with the integrity of that system. That major vendor now keeps in constant touch with us. When the present contract is up in about two years, the major vendor will be back with a very tough bid. In the long run we will get very competitive bids. It also works out for us because the small vendor is just going out of his way to be here a number of times each week. We had a number of machines that broke down, and they replaced them just like that. They are trying to keep on top of it."

STUDY QUESTIONS:

1. Was sticking to their promise -- One bid, one shot. We don't play games -- promise keeping or arrogance? Can virtuous conduct seem like arrogance?

2. For the storyteller, sticking to the company's promise meant no re-bidding. Did this promise rule out re-bidding under the circumstances in the story?

3. Substantial savings were lost because re-bidding was not permitted. Was it right for the storyteller to give up this opportunity to save money for the com-

pany? Does promise-keeping take priority over making a profit?

4. The storyteller concluded that sticking to their promise was good business practice. Do you agree?

5. Promise keeping was a long held value of the company. How would the discussion have gone between the purchasing manager and the storyteller without this long held tradition?

HIS WORD WAS GOOD

"I'd like to give you some background for an ethical dilemma we faced. Our company's primary business is banking, but one of our affiliates is a national provider of data services to financial institutions. In marketing these services, it is important that our company's other affiliates use the software and processing facilities of its data services affiliate ('data affiliate'). Few, if any, competitors of our data affiliate can boast this.

"I am employed by an affiliate that uses the services of our data affiliate. (I'll call my subsidiary the 'user affiliate') We are a regional leader in our field. Two years ago, we took a strategic look at our long term needs for data services from both client and operational perspectives. We sought to determine whether we were getting the best overall system from the data affiliate -- an operating system that could change with the developing needs of the 90's. Even raising this question put a cloud over the creditability of data affiliate's software. None the less, we needed to do this in order to maintain our competitive edge in a rapidly shifting industry.

"We compared our data affiliate's software with those of the four or five national competing software vendors. The vendors' managers and marketing 'reps' were concerned and cautious about our affiliate taking an unfair look at their software. After all, our data affiliate is their direct competitor; and they feared that we might be or could be conducting industrial espionage. We might be providing our data affiliate with inside information on what other systems can or can not do and how each of the systems went about its tasks of processing information.

"The president of our data affiliate initiated the review after exploring the matter with the chairman of the holding company. The president appointed a committee representing the various areas of the user affiliate, including client services and operations. He charged us with looking objectively at the data affiliate's systems and the vendors' systems, and at looking at their advantages, disadvantages and costs.

"He made it very clear that none of the information obtained from a vendor was to be conveyed to the data affiliate or another vendor in any way, shape or form. The president, himself, attended all the initial meetings with each of the vendors giving the message that his word was good -- the information would be treated with the utmost confidence. The practice of maintaining this type of confidence -- or creating a 'Chinese Wall' between affiliates of the same organization -- is not unusual in the financial services industry. (A 'Chinese Wall' is a set of beliefs and practices that stops the flow of particular information across units of an organization.) The review committee was responsible for keeping the president's word.

"At the end of the six month review, the committee met separately with each vendor and with our data affiliate; and the committee gave feedback on its assessment of each system's strengths and weaknesses. The committee recommended to the president that our user affiliates continue to employ the data affiliate's systems but also incorporate some subsystems of one or two vendors.

"Understandably the president of the data affiliate was pleased with our user affiliate's decision. He was also impressed and grateful for the feedback -- in general terms -- of how their software stood up with other software on the market.

Since the review, the data affiliate certainly has taken it upon itself to try much harder to provide customer support and more progressive programming at our request and has worked much more closely with our user affiliates. Some of the vendors got pieces of the business that they otherwise would not have had, although they did not get the prize.

"The real lesson here was that we were able to accomplish our objective of reviewing alternative systems and selecting the combination of products most suitable to us because of the President's insistence on confidentiality. I think we gained the respect of the various vendors, and we continue to work with some of them. It provided the opportunity to have the best operational system. Most importantly, it provided an ethical framework for our user affiliate in dealing with the corporate organization and its other affiliates. I believe that we would have selected an external vendor instead of our data affiliate if the review had warranted it. The tone set by the exercise of trust and confidentially made that possible."

STUDY QUESTIONS

1. The VP gave his word to competitors that neither he nor his task force would share competitors' information with his data affiliate. Did he have a right to withhold information that would benefit his company? Should he have broken his promise?

2. Was he being disloyal to his company by being trustworthy with competitors? Should managers withhold information about competitors from their own organizations whatever they promised?

3. Can information be prevented from flowing from one affiliate to another affiliates (departments, divisions or subsidiaries) without the tradition of a 'Chinese wall')?

4. The user affiliates needed information about the data affiliate's competitors for the user affiliates to evaluate their own competitive edge. On the other hand, they felt that it was wrong for them to collect this information by a ruse or industrial espionage. They resolved their dilemma by an elaborate procedure that maintained a 'Chinese wall' between themselves and the data affiliate. Do you agree with their ethical assumption that it was wrong to collect information about competitors by ruse?

5. Is industrial espionage wrong if it within the law?

6. Does promise keeping have a place in relations with competitors?

A SERVANT LEADER: THE STEADFAST TIN SOLDIER

Reflecting on the career of the College's vice president, the storyteller said, "I think he'd made a promise to himself that he was there to serve the religious order of nuns and that this was to be their institution. He was steadfast about never taking away their power but being there to empower them to run their college in spite of changing times. Loyalty and integrity were his way. His whole career was spent adhering to his promise -- keeping his promise."

The vice president was hired by a Catholic college and served as its vice president for more than 25 years -- during the tenure of three presidents who were sisters. When they hired him, the College was taking a first step that eventually changed its vision and culture radically. The College was then small, largely unknown in the region; but now it is the largest "small" college -- highly visible. From a single campus "hidden away" on valuable real estate, it now has sites in several states. Its vision changed from being inward looking, serving its small community of students and teachers to looking out into the region to serve a diversity of students and educational needs.

Founded to provide a liberal arts education and teacher training for members of its religious community, the college had expanded to enroll other women and later, men. The vice president was behind the move to coeducation and introduced basketball. [The sisters loved basketball and went to all the games. It was indoors and warm.] He launched the first publicity campaign to give the college visibility with a peppy slogan, targeting students.

The storyteller said, "The College's values remained much the same through the transition -- stressing poverty, simplicity and caring service; but the context for these values underwent profound change. This change came with glacier-like speed. The newer faculty and staff responded favorably to the pressures of serving a diversity of needs and locations, and their positive response gave rise to anxiety and tension among the traditional members of the community. Additional tension arose out of the College's efforts to obtain support from the greater nonsectarian community where the College was situated. The steps taken by the newly hired vice president foretold the transition and were feared."

I asked the vice president about these first steps. and he reflected on the person who was president at the time he was hired. He said "She was a truly religious woman -- aging but dedicated to the college and its people. The administrative team loved and supported her." The storyteller, however, said, "She was president of a community frozen in its past so hiring an outsider as vice president was fraught with anxiety."

The storyteller said, "The vice president stood between and connected two communities. One was the president along with other religious-order faculty -- living their commitment to poverty, humility and prayer. The other group -- wanting to serve a greater diversity of stakeholders -- were lay staff along with some sisters, alumni, new students and supporters from the City. The president was sensitive to the pain of the transition and hesitated to take steps to bring about change, while the college community was divided between some that held to the traditional ways and others who were restive over the slowness of change. Yet the president did provide a role model for embracing change -- cautiously -- with humility and caring for those threatened by its speed and those aggrieved by its slowness.

"He was the first male allowed in the 'inner sanctum' and he scared everybody. He was a big person, and just his walking through the hall sent shudders through the staff. He 'ruffled their robes.' The guy had to be so careful of every word and every mannerism so as not to draw attention to himself. He was courteous, gentle, sat with hands down on his lap, never pushed his feet out and always deferred to the president. He accompanied the president wherever she went; and he only spoke in her name, never for himself.

"Both camps challenged the vice president and blamed him for everything new that was happening and everything new that was not. The avant-garde saw many of the policies as detrimental to the development of the College, such as keeping 'tired, worn out courses, old fashioned materials and dull styles;' and they criticized him for not moving the College faster. The traditionalists faulted him for the changes. They disliked the noise -- the students, growing in number, sub-scribed to the college's values but not the traditional religious-orders demeanor. The noise was just another sign for the tra-ditionalists that the college was forgetting the virtues upon which the order was founded.

"He did not speak up to defend himself; but quietly en-couraged one camp to change and the other to be patient. 'The tail must not wag the dog,' he was fond of saying. I suppose each camp thought the other was the tail."

The storyteller was part of the avant-garde. She said, "Words such as 'money' carried negative connotations. So how do you pay your bills? How do you raise funds for future de-velopment? Displaying the college's strengths and needs went against the grain as did publicity and community relations. These were reserved and humble nuns who only knew one 'community', their religious community. They were as uncom-fortable 'boasting' about the college as they were about them-selves. How do you build a base for raising funds? How do you promote the college to potential students and donors?

"He hired me as the first community relations director; and, the day I was introduced, a wave of doubt and suspicion went through the staff. Afterwards, some bold sisters came to me, absolutely aghast, and asked, 'What community are you going to relate to?' How could I be their community relations director when I wasn't even in their order!

"The vice president intended that I be the College's first outreach to the metropolitan and business communities. Of course, he was not expecting me to relate to the religious or-der. He introduced my job as 'friend raising and fund raising' to bring about better understanding of my role. We couldn't say 'fund raiser' because that was an evil word. I and my work were greeted by misunderstanding and suspicion on the part of the staff. He absorbed the heat by receiving the concerns and never passing the blame to the president. Actually we gained support and trust after a while. I must credit forward minded sisters.

"One time I went to a major bank to ask for support. To my surprise, not one but three vice presidents greeted me. They were very curious about the College, its mission and its financial viability. They asked many probing questions about our annual financial report. They wanted to see if the institution ran in the red or black and if it had a cumulative deficit before investing their support.

"The College vice president called me a week later, 'Get your lunch and report immediately to the Blue Room.' The Blue Room was a private dining room usually reserved for meetings of the College's directors. The President and vice president were seated at a long dining table when I entered. The President was red faced and clearly upset when she opened the conversation. 'Why did you go out and talk with those strangers about these confidential matters?' she asked. Clearly, she felt the college's financial statements were private matters and I was out of line. The college had never shared its reports before.

"This was the only time that I met with the President in circumstances where my aggressive approach to community relations was questioned. Finally I saw exactly what heat I was creating in the sisters' community. The vice president, I came to realize, was absorbing it. Also he was absorbing criticism from me and other 'young professionals' who felt things were going too slowly. He never said, 'You can't because the sisters won't have it' or because 'this is their institution and they haven't allowed it.' He just absorbed the criticism. From them he got accusations that he was letting things get out of control. The pressure must have built up so that he had to let a little steam out by letting us meet one another directly.

"Here was a man with a 'code of loyalty' that said, 'you never say anything bad about your boss.' In all the years I knew him he never did. He steered the College through enormous changes, and the credit always went elsewhere."

"Major changes meant that control passed from the religious community to a lay governing board and faculty. The sisters accepted the consequences, and they made the tough decisions slowly, in their time, allowing the institution to handle it without severe pain, disruption or death. The College retained the heritage of the sisters and their community's values, although the mix of programs, faculty and students changed.

"The vice president brought the sisters and their college into the 20th Century, but he was not popular for this. He was not loved except by a few who were part of the President's Office and understood his dedication. The irony is that the new board members, 'latecomers to the changes', had no understanding of his contribution. They saw him sitting next to the president, and they dismissed him as a 'functionary'. That's giving up power -- the price of keeping a lifetime promise. That is what it means to be a steadfast tin soldier."

I asked the vice president what leadership looked like from the eyes of a steadfast tin soldier? He said, "Very few 'at court' are aware of what the #2 person does by way of sharing worries, offering ideas, suggesting changes, seeking solutions, composing letters, writing speeches, pacifying challengers, arranging agendas, mollifying enemies, cultivating friends -- and listening, listening, listening to the president because 'everybody needs somebody' who can identify, empathize and sympathize with them. I was privileged to move to the top of an organization with the person that became president and was privileged *to be friends* with her as well as our other professional associates. I found that our joint expenditure of time, talent, effort and energy was most productive and gratifying -- even if I seldom stood in the limelight. There are other motives here (beyond oneness in mind and heart) and that is the meritorious satisfaction of laboring together, 'doing the Lord's work'. For me and my respective sister presidents, we had the awesome opportunity of applying the sisters' religious values within a well respected institution. We held the college and its mission as our ministry."

He had kept his promise to himself that the College was to be their institution, reflecting their values. He had been their servant leader.

STUDY QUESTIONS

1. What promise did the vice president keep? Was this promise worth pursuing? Would it have been right to 'bend' his promise if it would have quickened the transformation of the organization?

2. The College successfully transformed itself. Was the vice president's leadership under the circumstances exemplary conduct or simply good management practice?

3. The vice president was the servant leader in the sense that his conduct was unassuming and self effacing.[1] Leadership for him was serving the president and the College. Was this role masking his exercise of power to radically change the institution? Or was he empowering others to accomplish these goals? Was he being manipulative or humble?

4. Was his self effacing conduct a matter of keeping his promise or a lack of self esteem?

5. Executives are often assertive, perhaps ruthless, in transforming their organizations. There is little tolerance for those that disagree with their direction. They often do not project the image of servant leaders. Is the servant leader an appropriate model for senior executives in business? Why or why not?

---

[1] "He did not cry or lift his voice or make it heard on the street...a bruised read he will not break...he will not fail or be discouraged till he has established justice in the earth." Isaiah 42:2-4, ibid., p. 873.

ACCEPTING RESPONSIBILITY WHEN THINGS GO WRONG

"I only observed this incident from afar and was not directly involved; but I was really affected by what happened as were other employees. We are a public utility, and much of our equipment is out in the field. Its purpose is to transmit electricity to our customers, and virtually everybody is our customer.

"Our CEO is relatively new in his position. Since becoming CEO, he has focused on empowering people, getting them to be accountable and working to their full potential. I've gone through a lot of training to instill these values in our organization. We're still working on it.

"We had an accident recently that shook everyone. I'm not clear on all the details but the overall situation was terrible. The accident involved a transformer that reduced the voltage of electricity as it flowed from the outside line to the apartment buildings. The transformer was housed in a metal box that sat on a concrete slab, and the box was locked with a padlock.

"Occasionally the equipment is vandalized. One if the things people do is cut off the padlocks for scrap value. Unfortunately, this particular transformer was vandalized, and the lock was missing. A child of five got into the box and was severely injured. As the hours passed, the company uncovered that someone had made a note on an inspection report that the padlock was missing. The division office gets hundreds and hundreds of these infraction reports, and it was just a note on the bottom. People process these reports -- all they do is input the reports into a computer and generate work requests. The missing padlock was not identified as a priority. It became clear that the Company had the information that the padlock was missing, and we had not taken any action to get the padlock back on.

"As soon as the CEO found this out, he went to the media and explained what happened. The CEO and other managers met with our attorneys, and the CEO concluded, after discussion, that it was our fault that this little boy was able to make contact with electric power. Often times there are danger signs on these things, but you can't expect a small child to read a danger sign.

"The CEO made a number of attempts to contact the family to express our sorrow; but I believe the family was advised by their attorney not to speak with the Company. None the less, we contacted the doctor to assure him that -- anything he needed -- we would pay for. It was not an issue.

"The CEO went to the press and apologized and said it was our fault that this happened. He took responsibility for the accident.

"That really sent a message to the employees. First, we felt really bad about it -- it was our Company, our product. I think all of us felt responsible in some way. He stood up and said he was accountable. This was a strong message on how to be accountable for something. I think accountability is demonstrated through our actions. It is better to stand up and accept ownership for what happened. You gain respect by doing that, not punishment. When the CEO made that statement, he probably felt that there was going to be a lawsuit. He could have said that the incident was beyond our control and made a variety of defenses. But he didn't do that. Actually they settled for a substantial sum. Of course we wished that the accident never happened because of the harm to the boy."

STUDY QUESTIONS

> 1. The storyteller saw a moral in this incident where the CEO kept the company's promise of being responsible for its actions. The CEO did not shift the blame to others. How did she relate this to her life and responsibilities?

2. Would the storyteller have felt betrayed if the CEO had not accepted responsibility in the Company's name? Why or why not?

3. The storyteller said, "It is better to stand up and accept ownership for what happened. You gain respect by doing that, not punishment." Do you think that it is better to accept responsibility when things go wrong? Why? Do you agree with the storyteller that you gain respect, not punishment by accepting ownership?

4. What should you do in situations where you know that you will be punished, not respected for accepting responsibility?

5. Some readers interpreted the company's actions as simply a matter of public relations. Whatever management's motives, what does the storyteller's interpretation say about her? Is she a person of integrity or simply naive?

6. What difference does it make in what the company did if the CEO was motivated by the gain from public relations or motivated with keeping the Company's promise?

STANDING FOR AUTONOMY[1]

Central to Margaret McGinnis' vision was the Trust Company's autonomy from the banking side of the Holding Company.[2] Margaret was the chief executive of the Trust Company. It was a free standing subsidiary of the Holding Company rather than a division within the Holding Company's flagship bank. As a subsidiary, the Trust Company has its own board of directors and capital structure, and it was autonomous from the banking side of the business.

As the chief executive, Margaret was faced with the need to uphold the Trust Company's autonomy in the face of pressure to fold it into the flagship bank. In defending this principle, she had to assess how far she should go as executive of the subsidiary in opposing a position of the holding company. For Margaret it was a matter of standing for a commitment that she and her predecessors had made. They believed that the complete separation trust and banking operations was the most effective way to operate a trust company.

The idea of autonomy developed over the history of the Trust Company. It was established in the late 1800's as a separate legal entity because national banks were not then permitted to exercise trust powers. Circumstances changed from time to time, and the question was raised on a number of occasions whether the Trust Company should remain autonomous or be a division of the flagship bank. New banking laws, changes in banking regulation, competitive pressures, capital needs and effective bank management opened the merger question as these circumstances arose. So there was a long term internal discussion and dialogue.

---

[1] This story is about the same person as "The Glass Ceiling" and "Obligations to Clients".

[2] Margaret McGinnis, Trust Company and Holding Company are fictitious names.

In response to this discussion, the executives at the Trust Company articulated and explained their belief that the Company should remain separate. Trust activities, they believed, were different from other banking activities; and commercial bankers did not understand the imperatives of trust operations. This belief was not unique to the Trust Company for it was the accepted view among some leading trust companies.

The commercial bankers did not necessarily share this view and offered counter examples. They had the impression that the trust side did not want to talk with them very much. As one officer of the flagship bank said, "They guarded their autonomy jealously."

Margaret was strongly committed to the Trust Company being a separate entity. An independent structure, she felt, would best attract and retain top flight people and would best act in the interests of its clients. She spoke to this belief of the Trust Company very persuasively and forcefully, and it has been part of the story told to new employees.

One officer, coming aboard after Margaret retired, said, "When I got to the Trust Company, I was told that being a separate trust company was not only unusual, but a real positive. We believe it; and we tell our customers that being a separate company is important in serving their needs. It makes sense to me and our customers. Many events in the financial communities over the last two decades strengthened our belief."

Several managers told me the story of her stance to maintain the autonomy of the Trust Company. She was seen as acting to prevent it from becoming a component of the Holding Company's flagship bank. Managers, joining the Company after Margaret's retirement retold the story. They said that there were a number of times over Margaret's career where there were attempts to dissolve the Trust Company and make it part of the banking structure. As they heard the story, she recognized the importance of autonomy and fought very effectively to maintain an independent structure."

A person on the scene at the time said, "There was a proposal, while Margaret was chief executive, to merge the Trust

Company into the flagship bank. A study had been done at the holding company, and a lot of work was done on it. Margaret was very upset about the proposal. She believed that it would be a terrible mistake. She did a study of her own and put together a 'white paper' on the subject explaining why she was opposed to making trust operations part of the flagship bank. Margaret was so convinced -- so convinced that it would serve everybody's best interest in the long run -- that she laid her career on the line. She said, 'I believe this so strongly that, if you do this, I'm going to resign.'

Another participant at the time said, "She was very courageous in standing up for the Trust Company when matters were questioned by the holding company. The Holding Company felt that the Trust Company should be merged into the flagship bank. The Holding Company's management discussed this with its board and raised the matter with Margaret. Some board members wondered about the wisdom of this but had not taken a great stand against it. The discussion was still underway when Margaret took the position that she would not be able to stay on if the Trust Company was merged with the bank. Management dropped the merger plans, and I think it was wise that it did so. The Trust Company has been independent ever since.

"This was an unusual position for a chief executive officer to take. She felt so strongly that a merger would be disastrous that she put her job on the line. She said go ahead and merge it, but I will retire. She was so important to the whole operation that the merger was dropped.

"People learned that, if there was an important enough question, you must be willing to face it head on and resign if you can't go along with the decision. Now most people hate to do that because they lose their jobs, and you know how important that is. I thought it was splendid what Margaret did."

Margaret said that she did not see herself facing the issue 'head on', but dealing with the matter quietly without confrontation. She said that she was told that plans were being made to merge the Trust Company with the flagship bank; and she said, "You know I can't stay if that happened." It was never raised with her again.

STUDY QUESTIONS

1. What makes autonomy of the trust operations so important that the chief executive risked her job for it?

2. What, if any, would be the harm in her giving in on this one issue? Was the issue only an organizational principle, or was the organization's culture at stake?

3. Some companies have their trust operations as subdivisions of their flagship banks. Considering the risk to herself, could she have 'backed off' based on the fact that some banks operate this way?

4. The story, "Standing for Autonomy" was part of the Trust Company's folklore and was retold to new employees. What impact would a story like this have on the culture? Generally, what do highly visible episodes of virtue or vice mean for an organization? Have you read or observed such episodes? What impact did they seem to have.

5. One officer said that it was unusual for a manager to propose to resign over a change in policy, and another said that her action was splendid. What do you think? Would you be prepared to resign under such circumstances?

WHAT IS A COMMITMENT WORTH

"I was working for a CEO, and I was the VP of Operations. We were looking to expand our finishing and distribution warehouse. Our space was no longer adequate. We were occupying 60,000 square feet in a building that could accommodate 120,000. We needed a minimum of 90,000 for the things that we wanted to do.

"The logical thing was just to expand at our current facility since the rest of the space was not occupied. However we thought that the landlord had set an arbitrarily high price. So we engaged consultants to identify other sites that would satisfy our needs, and we initiated negotiations with a competitor of our current landlord. The competitor gave us extremely attractive terms to take occupancy in their building. Even factoring the moving costs, we would save a considerable sum of money over the length of the lease. They just made a terrific proposal. The person who was negotiating with me went to his board and got approval for the bid.

"The competitor said, 'This is the offer. I need to have a commitment. Are you guys going to do this or not?' I sat down with my CEO and reviewed the terms with him. The CEO had been updated on a continuing basis on the status of negotiations. Our consultants said that this was a great deal, and we should act on it. The CEO said it was great, and it was the kind of deal we were looking for. It reflected what he thought the market price should be. He instructed me to go ahead and sign the letter of intent and that we were going forward.

"It was too bad that our current landlord wasn't willing to negotiate because, all things being equal, we would have preferred to stay in our present location. However, he had given us -- what he said -- was his bottom price, and he wasn't going to move. Therefore the competitor's bid was much more attractive.

"Our landlord's competitor told me that he wanted to come over to our offices and shake some body's hand on the deal. I asked my CEO if he was willing to do that. I said, 'Are you willing to shake the competitor's hand on the deal? He is looking for a personal commitment.' The CEO said, 'Absolutely. You can tell him to come over here. He's got a deal.'

"I telephoned the competitor to relay the message. He said, 'It is 4:30 in the afternoon. I'm going to take you guys at your word. Please sign the letter of intent.' So I faxed it to him. He added, 'Monday morning we'll start putting this thing together.'

"Monday morning rolled around. The current landlord found out that we were serious -- that we weren't bluffing. We were going to pull out. That created all sorts of consternation. Obviously, the current landlord started rethinking his strategy, and they realized that they had made a tactical error. They assumed that we wouldn't move, and now we were going to.

"The current landlord came back to us, and they put together a new deal for us that would save us about $100,000 over the four year life of competitor's bid, and it would save us close to $250,000-300,000 over their previous rock bottom bid. They came down very, very significantly.

"The CEO reviewed the situation, and he asked for my recommendation. I said, 'Well, quite honestly, as negotiators, we probably blew it.' I said that I take some of the responsibility for that. Obviously, we didn't communicate to them strongly enough that they were going to lose the deal if they did not give us a better price. That did not negate the fact that the competitor made a fantastic proposal to us. I signed a letter of intent based on the CEO's instructions. We all thought we had a good deal with the competitor. The landlord's current proposal is a better deal. Unfortunately, it came too late. We've made a commitment so we have to go with the commitment.'

"The CEO said, 'Well, I want to think about this over lunch.' He came back after lunch and said, 'You know, you're right. My honor is worth more than $100,000. We are going to stick with the deal that we made on Friday.'

"The landlord heard about this, and he proposed another deal. His new proposal -- instead of saving us $100,000 over

Stories of Virtue in Business

the four year life of the competitor's bid -- would save us
$200,000

My CEO reversed his position and justified his action:
'Well, I have a fiduciary responsibility to the ownership, and
we're going to break the deal.' He instructed me to call the
competitor and tell him that we were not going forward. There
was some legal liability because we signed the letter of intent,
but the CEO was confident that the competitor would not press
the issue because they didn't want the negative publicity anymore than we did.

"So somewhere between $100,000 and $200,000 was
what his honor was worth and his fiduciary responsibility
kicked in.

"I asked the storyteller what he thought about that. He
said, "I thought that it was the wrong decision. The CEO had
the right to be critical of me and the other people involved in
the negotiations as well as his own judgment on what terms
would clear the market. However we had made a commitment.
I personally had signed the letter of intent. The negotiations
were finalized, and someone coming along after that should
not have altered our commitment.

"We had a good deal. We were not a company in absolutely dire economic straits where every dollar meant we were
going to keep one more person on the payroll. We were not in
that kind of situation at all. It did impact the bottom line.
Obviously, it had financial implications, but it wasn't something that was going to make or break the company or even the
financial year. With regard to our total sales volume, it wasn't
going to have a perceptible impact."

"I asked the storyteller what lesson he drew from this incident. He said, "What it drove home to me is that with regard
to the CEO, every commitment was going to judged against its
financial implications. He had a financial limit on what his
word was worth. I don't think that things should be that condi-
tional. There are some things that should be absolute. He did
not have any absolutes. A commitment is final."

"I asked him about what it meant for himself. He said,
"Number one, my decision was that I needed to get out of this
situation. This was not a relationship where I was going to be

comfortable over the long run. This was from a personal standpoint. Secondly, I learned something. You have to be crystal clear so that the other person understands what I'm telling them -- You're going to lose the deal and that they really understand that. If I had been clearer with the landlord, this possibly might not have occurred."

And I asked him, so you left the company?

'I left the company. This was one situation. There were others where my judgment call on ethical matters were different from the CEO's."

STUDY QUESTIONS

1. Compare this story with "Sticking to Our Promise'. What were the rationales the storytellers gave for keeping their commitments?

2. In both stories, the storytellers made commitments to suppliers. How did they balance their commitments to their suppliers with the rights of owners?

3. The storyteller said that a commitment was absolute (final). He also suggested hypothetical financial conditions where backing out of a commitment was understandable. Do you agree or disagree? Why?

4. The storyteller said that honor had a financial limit for his CEO. Do you think honor -- living virtuously -- has a financial limit?

5. Would you leave a company, as the storyteller did, because of incidents such as the one described in the story? Explain.

PART VII

ACTING WITH COMPASSION

Compassion does *not* mean pity or sentiment about the plight of another as used here. Pity and sentiment are worthy feelings, and they often accompany compassion. Compassion is an awareness of togetherness.[1] Compassionate people know that they are interconnected with other people and their mutual environment. They rejoice in another's joy and grieve in another's sorrow, and they seek justice and care for others. The virtue of compassion is characterized by a life style where one is aware of the impact one has on another.

> "No man is an island, entire of itself; every man is a piece of the continent, a part of the main; if a clod be washed away by the sea, Europe is the less, as well as if a promontory were, as well as if a manor [house] of thy friends or of thine own were; any man's death diminishes me, because I am involved in mankind; and therefore never send to know for whom the bell tolls; it tolls for thee."[2]

Business men and women, like everybody else, can act with compassion. They can live a deep awareness of their togetherness with others. There is often a difference, however, in the circumstances where they practice this virtue. In their

---

[1] Matthew Fox, *A Spirituality Named Compassion and the Healing of the Global Village, Humpty Dumpty and Us* (Minneapolis: Winston Press, 1979), pp. 1-35.

[2] John Donne, *Devotions*, XVII, 1624, Bartlett, op. cit., p. 218a.

business role, they exert substantial influence over economic activity generally and, in particular, over the operations of enterprise. They provide the leadership for manufacturing, banking, hospitals and other economic enterprise; and they directly influence the economic and social well-being of enterprise. Executives are astride the stakeholders, and play an important role in balancing their interests. The stakeholders' interests can be conflicting and *not* mutually attainable.

Thus business men and women impact economic activity, the fate of their enterprises and balance of stakeholder interests. They make decisions and take actions that sometimes bring suffering and other times bring good outcomes. The circumstances where they operate give wider scope to their decisions than the decisions of most people. Consequently, executives need to have an awareness of people and the environment that is more comprehensive.

Compassionate business people stand with and do what they can for those that suffer and celebrate with those that have good times. Compassion does not mean to procrastinate or evade decisions that may have harmful, as well as beneficial, outcomes; rather, it implies the courage to act and redress the negative effects as well as one can. To be compassionate, executives need to understand the consequences of their decisions for others and their environment; they need to act with courage out of their best judgments; and they need to be generous in helping those that are harmed by their decisions.

Many of the stories were about actions where compassion was an element; however, compassion -- or its lack -- is the predominate theme in the stories in Part VII. Four stories are told in this part: "Downsizing"; "A Helping Hand"; "Compassionate Hospitals" "ESOP"; "Corporate Compassion"; "You're Fired"; "No Guardian Angel"; "A Little Bit Disappointed"; and "Cold Hearted".

DOWNSIZING

"Downsizing" is a brief story. A compassionate manager muses about the action he took in terminating employees because his company was implementing a downsizing strategy. He was given a mandate to reduce the number of employees, and he believed that he is compelled to downsize to remain competitive. Nonetheless he empathized with those terminated. Supported by company policy, he helped them in their predicament; and expressed the belief "that it is the right thing to do -- the ethical thing".

A HELPING HAND

"A Helping Hand" is another brief story about compassion -- and about mentoring. The storyteller relates how he was helped in his professional development and career by his boss who was his mentor. Now the storyteller expresses compassion for his staff and makes himself available to help them.

COMPASSIONATE HOSPITALS

"Compassionate Hospitals" is about the generation and destruction of compassion in the organization's culture. The story takes place in a chain of specialty hospitals where the major owner and a group of senior managers were facilitating a climate of compassion among the staff and stakeholders. The story is told from the perspective of the Vice President of Human Resources who is a leader in the 'reengineering' of the climate. He tells his story about the company's vision that people count, and he relates what was done to imbue the organization with compassion. He is dedicated to the owner and supportive of the owner's efforts to change the hospital' climate. The owner, however, is not clear on what constitutes compassion in the hospitals' circumstances and seems driven more by 'ego' than compassion.

A couple of years after the end of the story, in a postscript, the storyteller tells the interviewer that he has contracted a catastrophic illness. Two days after he informed the CEO of his illness, his position was eliminated; and he was fired. Virtue is fragile even with resolve.

ESOP(Employee Stock Ownership Plans)

ESOP is a story about two principal owners who sold their company to the employees. The principals were concerned for the employees' welfare as they approached retirement and wanted to insure the continuation of the company and the employees' jobs. They felt that the employees would only be protected by establishing an ESOP. The principals considered selling it to outside interests, but found that the new investors would cut pay and relocate facilities out of the state. This was unacceptable to the principals so they arranged a transfer of ownership to the employees.

The principal owners also wanted to insure a fair deal for the other stockholders while avoiding too much leverage as a consequence of the buy out. The principals negotiated a bank loan to buy all stock including their own, but they then reinvested their portion in the company as preferred stock. The preferred stock would be repurchased by the company over a period of time. They did this to protect the liquidity of the company and to insure its continuing success and the employees' jobs.

The story also speaks to their generosity over a lifetime.

CORPORATE COMPASSION

The story is about two incidents where employees were disabled by long term illness. These incidents occurred before the enactment of the Americans with Disabilities Act, and the business corporation in the story was not required to accommodate these employees. However, its approach and tradition was to assist employees with disabilities.

In the first incident, the employee contracted multiple sclerosis (MS). His mental functioning slowed down, and he became much less productive. He was unable to get disability compensation, however, because of the difficulty in getting the government to certify him as disabled. The Corporation responded by first redefining his job into 'bite sized' chunks so the disabled person could do the work. Secondly, it retained a lawyer to present the case to the Social Security Administration and have the person certified as disabled. The employee got certification; and, when the person could no longer function in his job, he was then able to get disability compensation.

The second incident involved a person whose disability required that he obtain extensive treatments at a hospital to continue to function. In this situation, the Corporation allowed him to take whatever time was necessary to take the treatments and, still, to continue in his job. The employee was able to work while taking the treatments and gave more hours to his work than expected, but the Corporation did not know this and was prepared to continue his employment.

YOU'RE FIRED

Jack, the newly hired divisional controller uncovered what he suspected to be a problem. Material was being shipped from his division to a business owned by the divisional president, and the divisional president's business was supposed to ship back the finished apparel. However Jack had no record of what happened to the finished apparel. The divisional president was a substantial stockholder because he had been a principal owner when this division was purchased with the holding company's stock. Also the divisional president sat on the board of the holding company.

Jack informed the holding company's chief financial officer and informed the divisional president of his investigations. That day, returning from lunch, Jack found a letter on his desk from the divisional president, firing him. Jack called the chief financial officer who told him that the division president did not have the authority to do that. The story, then, describes the repercussions of these events.

NO GUARDIAN ANGEL

The protagonist left his company and went back to school to get an MBA. Afterwards, he had jobs with two other companies Then he applied for a position at the company where he worked before graduate school. The story describes his feelings about what went into the company's decision to hire him. He thinks that he has no 'guardian angel' in the company to help him.

A LITTLE BIT DISAPPOINTED

A former student tells how he was passed over for promotion, and the son-in-law of the senior vice president was promoted instead. The story describes the senior vice president's justification and the reaction of the former student. The issues raised in the story involve compassion, trust and fairness.

COLD HEARTED

A CEO reflects on how difficult it is for him to fire someone, and he gives an example of an alcoholic who had been recovering, but is drinking again. He explains that he thinks that he is a better businessman for having compassion and not insulating himself from people in his organization.

DOWNSIZING

"The situation, being what it is, I had to reduce the number of employees; otherwise, I would not remain competitive. I guess many companies have the same trouble.

"I've worked out early retirement packages with five employees over the last three years. They apply for social security at age 62, and company provides them part-time employment and health insurance until age 65. Then they go onto Medicare and full retirement. Their compensation during the three years before 65 is about the same as after retirement.

"It allows them to wind down with part-time employment, reaching 65 more relaxed. It also lets them go away with their heads held high because, in some cases, technology has somewhat passed them by; and they are struggling, to say the least. So I'm able to let them retire with a good feeling about themselves. At the same time, I lower my payroll costs and bring in some new, younger programmers, or whatever I need to keep things going.

"I think that's the right thing to do, the ethical thing. I could be harsh and say to these people that they are no longer 'cutting it', and let them go. It is hard to do that to a person when they are getting older. We owe it to them. I'd rather spend additional money for those three years. Three years go so fast. I like to let them move on and make the most of their lives."

STUDY QUESTIONS

1. The storyteller believed that he was compelled to downsize, to remain competitive; yet he was compassionate with those that were being let go. He helped them in their predicament although at greater cost to the firm than if he had terminated them. Did he do the right thing? Should he have terminated them instead?

2. Was he justified in using the company's resources to maintain their benefits and partial employment instead of terminating them?

3. Did his action result in a substantial resolution of their predicament or was it a token effort?

4. What do you think is the place of compassion in business decisions? Do you think business leaders should be aware of their "togetherness with people" who are harmed by downsizing?

5. What actions should business leaders take to help those that are 'downsized'? Or does the responsibility rest on those 'downsized'?

6. What does it mean for business leaders to live a life of compassion?

A HELPING HAND

"Early in my career, a number of years ago, I was looking to break into a management position. I had been in a technical position relating to law and finance in the health services field, and I had changed companies; but my job was much the same. For about three months, I had been working for this fellow who was the director of finance. He told me that he was going to apply for the executive director position that meant his old position, director of finance, would be open.

"He knew of my interest in breaking into management and wanted to give me an opportunity to take a crack at the finance directorship. At the time neither one of us had a CPA, and he still had some concerns about that. I did not have my MBA at that time but had about five or six years of financial work experience. What he offered me was to fill the position on a temporary basis and without the title. I would keep my old title and salary level. He said that we would keep this arrangement until he felt comfortable promoting me. He was honest about where we stood. He said that he couldn't offer me any promises or more money. He felt certain that he could find someone with better qualifications and experience that would knock me out of the running if he recruited for this position. He did not want that to happen because he thought highly of me and felt that I would do a superior job. He had confidence in me.

"He was genuinely sincere, honest and supportive as a manager. If he made a commitment, he made sure it happened. In a sense, he took a risk in putting me in that position. I might have failed miserably, and he would have been in a big predicament; but he had confidence in me and was willing to guide and direct me.

"His conduct stands out. The flip side also stand out for other managers I've seen. They make promises that are empty. They tell you that you will be considered if you fill in. You do your old job and new job and put in an excellent performance, but the promise isn't sincere. I've seen this happen quite a bit, even in our own organization, where honesty is a cherished value.

"I viewed him as a mentor and have tried to follow his example of making my self available to other people. Some people say that they are available but actually are not. He was not perfect by any measure. There were a lot of things about his character that people didn't like. I admired him. He looked out for others and helped them.

"It's my belief, and I think his too, that you surround yourself with good people and develop them as experts to facilitate the job getting done. I tell my people that I am a resource and make myself available to them. Some managers are afraid to develop people for fear they will participate in a power play against them sometime down the road. He would not let fear of that possibility prevent him from doing the right thing."

STUDY QUESTIONS

1. The storyteller talked about his boss, the former director of finance, who became the executive director. This man had compassion for those who worked with him and for their career aspirations. He helped the storyteller develop his expertise so the storyteller could take over the position of director of finance. Did the executive director do the right thing? Should he have recruited from the outside instead? (The storyteller said that the executive director could have found someone more qualified that the storyteller.)

2. The storyteller is a mentor to his staff following in the footsteps of the executive director who mentored him. The storyteller also expressed regret about managers that are fake mentors and don't keep their promises to help their staff develop professionally. Does the storyteller -- and anybody for that matter -- have a right to be mentored? Does he have an obligation to mentor others because he was helped?

3. Is mentoring a matter of luck and a privilege -- or is it a matter of justice? Why or why not?

4. What role does compassion play in mentoring?

COMPASSIONATE HOSPITALS

"When I got a call from a search firm about this job and this company, I was not interested at all; but they were very persistent. I went to a series of interviews and ultimately had dinner with the board of directors and chairman. The chairman arrived late and immediately sat down right across the table from me. He looked at me and said, 'Why in the world would you want to work for a little organization like ours? And what makes the difference?' I looked at him and said, 'People make the difference.' He had a big smile on his face and said, 'That was the right answer.' He then asked if that difference ever stopped. I said, no, it was a never ending process of people and organization.' Again, he looked at me; he looked at my wife. He said that he wanted me to know that his company was a family. Family included patients and their families as well as staff. 'If you join the company', he said, 'you and your wife would be family.'

"There is always an element of compassion in the company. As director of human resources, I can have a check cut for up to $2000 to be lent to an employee without interest, and it is repaid as the employee's situation allows. The purpose is to get the person through hard times such as 'the gas company is going to turn off the heat' or 'my husband left me and took all the money.' The wage for many of our support service employees is five dollars an hour because of the industry's economic structure.

"My wife was pregnant and developed scarlet fever. When the chairman found out, he asked how she was doing. He said that he knew an expert in Atlanta and he would charter a plane to have her see this doctor. Well, we had things under control; and, in fact, nothing came of it. But that is the type of thing he does.

"A fourteen year-old daughter of a clerk had a terrible, terrible jaw problem. It was truly messed up by the doctors that had taken care of her. The chairman just said that he knew an expert; he wanted her to go and see him; and he would pay for everything. He told her not to worry over things the insurance wouldn't cover. He's always there for people regardless of what the situation may be.

"Compassion pervades the organization. Employees treat our patients as family. There have been instances where employees have taken home the laundry of patients' families. They come from all over, so these folks fly long distances and sometimes only have limited amount of clothing with them. Also employees will invite patients' family members home with them for a home cooked meal or whatever.

"It is not as if other people don't have different views and can't be anything but successful with us. We have people in the organization who don't necessarily live and breath and sleep this. It grates against some folks. These people can be successful for a period of time, but the fit isn't comfortable.

"A person in a very, very senior position had been with the organization for about two months. He headed up a company that we started. He was very brusque in his conversations with me. So I finally asked him if there was something wrong. He asked why I asked the question. I told him that was what he was communicating to me. I told him that I could take it, but that he was going to give all sorts of people the wrong idea. He's changed now with a more caring style. I don't think that he's changed on the inside; but he has, at least, changed on the outside.

"We have another CEO on the West Coast who is the most control oriented person I know. But he is successful and has made things happen. He's very lucky that he has an executive team and one key executive reporting to him who carries the passion for employees and customers forward and makes things happen.

"Something else our chairman requires is that all executives visit patients when we are in one of our facilities. You might expect this for executives in the sales-end of the business, but here I am the HR executive, and my job gives me no direct interaction with patients. Yet, I'll walk into patients' rooms and say, 'Hi, I'm Jack, Vice President of Human Resources. Is there anything I can do for you?' I visit a while.

"The other day, I was walking down a hospital corridor and saw several people using a pay phone. They were crying so I walked up and asked if I could help. They had put their mother in a van and had driven all the way from upstate New York to our hospital in the Midwest. Their mother had been given less than two weeks to live by a doctor back home. They were just beside themselves. I had them calm down. I made a point of visiting the patient and her family every week for a while. I sent flowers once the patient was doing a little bit better. It is just what we have been asked to do. I'm not unique as the HR executive. The chief financial officer does the same thing.

"Firing employees is a hard thing to do since they are family. Actually a month after I was hired, I found myself in a situation where we had to terminate someone -- an executive who'd been with the company for eight years. This was a person who had been through a messy divorce and, quite frankly, was having some emotional and psychological problems. We took care of the executive economically, providing counseling and anything and everything we could do to make sure that she was okay. She'd gone through all these personal devastating catastrophes, and now she was facing one more. Then there was the case of the president of the holding organization who didn't work out and had to be terminated. These are difficult situations.

"We had a situation about two years ago where a male middle manager sexually harassed female employees. The first time he abused an employee was before I joined the organization. I don't even think that they slapped him on the hands because it was a pretty chauvinistic organization, and still is in many quarters. The second time, I was there. I recommended termination, but the chairman's decision was to suspend the manager. Six months after that, the manager touched a female employee. There were witnesses and two court trials involved in this thing. We settled short of trial in federal court.

"After the settlement, I was at a board meeting; and I was asked by the chairman to give a report on the state of any labor relations issues. I gave a report on this case, and he asked what my conclusions were. I said that the man should be fired. We just settled out of court two days before this board meeting. I said that he was a menace to the organization. He was a menace to our employees. The chairman looked at me and said, 'maybe we should think of a different job for him. The man is fifty years old; he's worked for the organization for eighteen years; he's obese; and no one would hire him. We can't fire him. We have to find a job for him where he can't hurt anybody. If he can't perform in that job, then that's fine. But we have to give him one more chance.' I was disappointed. I thought that this man had received more chances than he deserved. But he got one more chance, and so we developed a job for him where he had no contact with employees. He was not successful with that, and before six months were up, he actually left on his own accord. Again, here is the chairman showing compassion for people. As I said before, his attitude seems to trickle down and pervade the organization.

"I'm committed; but, at times, I'm a doubting Thomas. We are financially very successful. Our experience has convinced me that we can deliver service and be more successful than you could ever dream of being. My commitment comes because I get more than a pay check. My work doesn't directly touch the patient, but I feel it does indirectly. If you've ever known someone that has a chronic disease and seen the family suffer through that -- if you can help in some way -- that's of great value and great personal satisfaction to me.

"Yet I can not help but wonder -- when I look at the growth of the business -- whether we will sell it some day. We know that it will be sold this decade, because we will have brought it to a point where it's just about as big as we are going to get it. When you are as passionate about delivering service as we are, there's some conflict in talking about selling. You might want to continue riding it on and on.

"In my mind, I struggle with the question whether our business can be sold and the organization continue to be compassionate. Would selling the business bring compassion to an end? I can't find a resolution. We are a for-profit business. If I had to define, in one sentence, what we are: we are in the business of providing the very best in-patient care available in the world. But it is a business. So I've reconciled that it is truly a business, and this is not a religious order that is going to perpetuate the hospital. It is in the hands of the new owners once it is sold. Life here will depend on their conduct. The chairman who has ownership control is an entrepreneur, and it is not his nature to stay with one business forever."

POSTSCRIPT

A couple of years later, I met Jack who had told the story about the compassionate hospitals. He said, "I've been fired. A few months ago, I was diagnosed as having a neurological illness that progresses slowly over many years to disable the person. I informed the chief executive and the chairman; and, two days later, my position was abolished.

"The company had grown spectacularly. Its core business had been hospitals for serious illnesses, but it diversified into other healthcare related industries several years ago. The chairman retained his position as chairman, and a new person was hired to take his duties as chief executive. The culture began to change with no clear focus at the corporate level, and executives no longer shared a common vision. Most key executives had left the company as a consequence, leaving me and the Medical Director as the only executives serving for more than four years.

"My job was reclassified from VP-Human Resources to VP-Recruitment to accommodate the company's expansion. I spent 95% of my time traveling nationwide to fill the new executive positions, and the HR function no longer had an experienced leader. Employee relations shifted from a participative model to an adversarial one. Although patients still received good care, the earlier family culture was gone.

"I convinced the chairman to put me back in the corporate HR function to address the erosion of employee relations, but I didn't have a chance to start the new job. I learned that I had this catastrophic disease that the company chose not to accommodate. I am able to perform the essential duties of this job, but my position was abolished two days after I told them.

I had received a 25% increase in pay just before this. Performance was not an issue."

STUDY QUESTIONS

1. The Chairman said that the Company was a family. What does "family" convey about the culture of their hospitals?

2. Is a life of compassion -- an awareness of their connection with one another-- an ideal for family? An ideal for the organization in the story/

3. The storyteller (the Vice President of Human Resources) was told that he and his spouse would be members of the company's family when he was hired. Was he treated as family?

4. The storyteller said that compassion pervaded the organization, and he described several episodes to illustrate exemplary conduct and a compassionate culture:
> a. Employees treated patients as family;
> b. A very senior executive modified his behavior to communicate compassion;
> c. Executives visited patients and offered their help;
> d. A woman with a messy divorce was terminated after psychological counseling and other support;
> e. A manager was not terminated after a number of instances of sexual harassment but was given additional opportunities to modify his behavior.

Do these episodes convey compassion -- that the organization lived an awareness of their connection with each other?

5. The storyteller raised the issue: "When you are passionate about delivering service as we are, there's some conflict in talking about selling...Would selling the business bring compassion to an end? I can't find a resolution." What is your judgment?

6. Was it appropriate to terminate the Vice President of Human Resources under the circumstances? Should his disability be a factor in the decision? Explain.

7. Would you expect the culture of compassion to survive the termination of the Vice President of Human Resources?

8. Was the Chairman a compassionate man? If not, how do you explain his acts of generosity? If he was, how do you reconcile compassion with the organization's termination of the divorced woman and the disabled executive?

9. From the story, it would seem that virtue is fragile and vice long lasting? Do you agree? Disagree?

ESOP[1]
(Employee Stock Option Plans)

The Chairman and Vice President were major stockholders and had a controlling interest in the Company. They were looking ahead to their retirement and decided to sell the Company and explored terms with a number of potential buyers. However, they encountered conflict between their values and the buyers' interests. One of the perspective purchasers, for example, wanted the Company to reduce salaries, wages and fringe benefits, and also talked about moving the plant out of Wisconsin. The Chairman and Vice president were not interested in arrangements of that kind so they decided to go the ESOP route and to sell the Company to the employees.

The person, telling the story, said, "The Chairman and Vice President were sincerely interested in the employees. When they put their decision to the employees over 92% voted in favor of accepting their ESOP proposal.

"As part of the transaction, they put up their own equity to make sure that the Company would remain here and remain profitable. They did this by using their own securities as collateral. Technically, their shares were bought out for cash as was everyone else's. But, in turn, the Chairman and Vie President accepted preferred shares instead of cash. These shares were to be retired in installments over a period of years. The Company was able to borrow substantially less as a result, strengthening the balance sheet and reducing debt service.

"Actions like this speak louder than words. They put their money on the line to accomplish something that they felt very strongly about and that has benefited everyone here."

An apocryphal story -- I heard from several managers -- was about a conversation between the Chairman and a group

---

[1] This story is about the same person as "Honesty as an Executive Style".

of investors. "The investors were willing to pay a very good price but expected the principals to continue to operate the Company since they didn't know how to run a 'smoke stack' manufacturing company. They wanted the Chairman and Vice President to re-negotiate their union contracts downward and wanted lower costs for salaried people before buying the Company. In talking to them, the Chairman said 'Well, if you tried to do that, half the people are going to quit, and it will be the best half.' Also the investors said that they would probably move its manufacturing facilities to one of their other plants where they had excess capacity. In response to moving the facilities, the Chairman said, 'Well then, as soon as you move the plant, you're going to lose the other half. You have already admitted that you don't know how to run the Company, so just what do you think you are buying.' Based on that, he simply said to them that he didn't think it was a deal that could work. The idea of outside investors moving the facilities out of this area disturbed the Chairman and Vice President very much so they came up with the idea for an ESOP."

The storyteller said, "All the employees know that they're working for themselves. We have to work together; and the longer that we're at this, the better job we do. In the long run, the more profitable we are, the more money we put into our pocket. It's to every one's benefit to work together. I think, at least from my standpoint, I appreciate what has been done here."

One manager implied, however, that the tax advantages entered into the decision to establish an ESOP. Of course there is always a flip side to interpreting conduct as exemplary. The view of the storyteller and the other managers was that this was a generous act and reflected their compassion for the employees.

The storyteller said, "The Chairman and Vice President were seen as persons who helped others, and were generous not only with their time but their expectations. When you're starting out, they don't expect you to work miracles. You find on the day you start that you have a learning period. Their willing to give a person a chance. I'm sure they watch to see what progress is made. They work hard and expect the same from others."

Another manager said, "They'll work with people; help them. They expect them to do a good job, consistent with their abilities; but they also realize that everybody's human, and errors occur. If anything, they demand that you do the best that you can. Whatever those results may be, good or bad. And not to shade things.

"People can talk to them about their problems. The Chairman will help employees that you would not think would ever talk to someone at his level in the organization. I know people who have talked with him about financial matters or legal matters, which were not related to the company's business. [The Chairman is an attorney] He's willing to listen. One case was a settlement related to a divorce. The letters you get from the court can be quite intimidating; and the Chairman would find out for the individual what the court really means as opposed to what they appear to say. In his years at the Company, the Chairman has given free legal service - within limitations of time - to all employees."

STUDY QUESTIONS

1. What were some indications of the Chairman and Vice President's compassion for the employees?

2. One manager was skeptical about the generosity of the Chairman and Vice President in selling the Company to the employees. He mentioned tax considerations. Other managers saw this as a generous act. What do you think?

3. The story indicated that the Chairman and Vice President had a lifelong habit of helping the employees. Could they have taken an offer for the Company that did not protect the employees jobs? Where is the virtue if it can be turned off and on?

CORPORATE COMPASSION

"I thought, maybe, I would start at the end and work to the beginning of the story. There is a reason for that. Just recently, Congress passed and enforced the Americans with Disabilities Act that applies to all major corporations. It addresses the hiring, firing, and promotion of people with disabilities, and it requires that corporations make accommodations for people with disabilities under certain circumstances. Corporations are now more aware of the need to accommodate people with disabilities; but, before this act, there were very few things on the books that could enforce these procedures.

"I say this now because it may not be unusual for corporations to do these things that are required under the Act; but I want to talk about two incidents before the Act. The particular corporation -- where the incidents occurred -- was not required to accommodate disabled people at that time. The incidents occurred before there was a law requiring their accommodation. Nonetheless this corporation made a very genuine and committed effort to assist disabled persons in its work force.

"It was never even a question for the CEO of this large publicly held corporation whether they should accommodate disabled persons. There was no internal debate about what the company should do. Management saw it as the compassionate -- the right thing -- to do. This view has continued to the present under four successive CEO's.

"The first incident involved a Vietnam War veteran who contracted MS (Multiple Sclerosis). He thought that his illness was related to some chemicals that were used in the war where he had received a medal for heroism.

"As I understand it, MS can move at any pace. It can be an extremely lengthy period before the person becomes totally disabled, or it can move very rapidly. MS can take many forms and have its effect over different periods of time. In this case it had moved very rapidly as far as affecting the guy's mental capabilities, but very slowly in affecting his physical motor capabilities. If you saw him walking down the hall, you couldn't tell anything was wrong; but it became pretty evident that something was awry if you sat down to talk with him. When you looked at his production, it was obvious that something was wrong. He was a very committed employee, almost zealously committed to his job. For him to be an under producer -- was beyond the realm of comprehension. You couldn't imagine it, so you knew something was wrong.

"The subtle effects of MS can make it difficult to recognize that an individual has a disability in MS' early stages. They are not immediately seen. It can be slow or fast moving but ultimately it is a totally disabling disease. In this person's case, he'd come to work and have a list of things that he wanted to do that day. He'd feel capable of doing them; but his mental faculties were slowing down so he'd find himself, maybe, with only two things completed of the ten that he expected to do. He just couldn't perform them as quickly; and as the day wore on, he became mentally tired so he slowed up.

"MS is the type of disease for which disability compensation is available. You can get long term disability compensation through the Corporation that provides 70% of salary for the time you are disabled. The problem was that the Corporation's policy was tied to the Social Security Administration's certification of disability. For you to get long term disability compensation, you had to be certified by the Social Security Administration as being totally disabled. What we discovered was that this was a very, very difficult certification to get. You almost have to be incapable of doing anything at all in your life. It is a very tough test; and with a creeping disease like this, you look very normal.

"His physical motor responses are just as clear and quick as if he had no disease, but it began by attacking his mental processes. So with this type of condition, it's very hard to be certified by the Social Security Administration as disabled. Since he couldn't get certification, he couldn't get long term disability from his company.

"The Corporation did some research into the problem and decided that they would try first to accommodate this employee in the work place. So they did a rigorous study of this person's workload and job description and pared it down to bite-sized chunks that he could handle.

"He did so in the beginning; but, as the disease progressed over the next two years, he became less and less able to handle very much of anything. In the meantime, he had gone down to the Social Security Office and started the process of trying to become certified as disabled; but he had not been certified thus far. So the Corporation, of its own volition, hired an attorney who specialized in dealing with the Social Security Administration to help this employee become certified. At its own expense, the Corporation incurred substantial legal fees in order to help this fellow. That took four or five months. After that, with a lot of work by the attorney, the employee was certified as disabled, and he received his long term disability from the Corporation. He was very grateful and pleased, and he has been back to the Corporation a number of times to thank the Corporation for what they had done for him. He even highlighted what they did for him in the MS Association. For me, it is an example of a company going the second mile.

"The same Corporation had another employee who contracted a disease that required him to have a number of treatments per week at a local hospital. As long as the employee received these treatments, he could function as a full time, competent worker. If the employee didn't receive these treatments, not only could he not function; but, after a period of time, it was a terminal situation.

"The employee wanted to work instead of going on disability so the Corporation arranged for him to leave at 3:30 PM in the afternoon, three days a week to have these treatments. They also made accommodations when tests had to be run. That lasted for a period of about seven years.

"As it worked out, the employee took his office work with him to the hospital and could actually work while these treatments were being administered. These were three hour treatments. The Corporation wasn't losing hours. As a matter of fact, they may have been picking up an hour or so as far as work load goes; but they did not know that.

"The Corporation, at the very outset, was willing to say: if you need to leave at 3:30, leave at 3:30 to get treatments; and you can work as long as you are able to work.

"So I guess my point is: long before the law required companies to accommodate and nurture, if you will, employees with severe disabilities, this Corporation was stepping up to the plate and making every effort to accommodate disabled employees. These two incidents are ones that I am familiar with, but I know there are others. I've seen a number of people in wheel chairs who are fairly severely disabled that are working here. Although the policy was not written, it was an unwritten commitment to the disabled, and they knew it. The commitment started at the top (CEO) and extended through management."

I said to the storyteller that someone who had read my stories told me that a compassionate person could not be trusted to assume managerial responsibility. This reader believed that a person of integrity would not be trusted with power. Yet, I said, you are describing a situation where the CEO and his successors were compassionate.

The storyteller said, "That's correct! Successive CEO's, who were entrusted with power, acted with compassion; and the Corporation's management acted with compassion. One of the reasons that this was true was that the persons with ultimate power, were committed to helping the less fortunate in the Corporation.

"If you had a situation where the person with the ultimate power, the chairman or president or both, were **not** so inclined, then I think it would be difficult to do the types of things I'm talking about here.

"Take this scenario: Let's just say the chairman of the board was not inclined to make concessions, but the vice president of sales had two disabled people that he wanted to help. My guess is that the vice president of sales -- if he was a person of integrity and if he was committed to helping these people -- would do so within the framework of his division. However, he would understand that there would be a point reached where he could go no further-- knowing his superiors' lack of compassion.

"As a 'for instance' -- I'm guessing that in that particular scenario [VP compassionate, but superiors not compassionate], as it relates to the two situations -- then the hypothetical vice president of sales could make an accommodation to the person that was going for treatments with the understanding that he would do his work while he was taking treatments and then the company would lose nothing. My guess is that, as far as the person with MS, -- the vice president could accommodate that person within his department as far as his workload, but the vice president could not hire an outside attorney to help the employee with the Social Security Administration.

"I guess what I'm saying: as long as the hypothetical vice president took actions internal to his group, he probably could help these people. However, if it involved expense to the company and something unusual like hiring an attorney, then he would probably feel that he couldn't do it because it was going against the wishes of the chairman in a way that would be detected. So he would be at risk.

"So the bounds where management can act with integrity does depend on the chairman or president. The hypothetical vice president of sales could help the disabled person within the confines of his own division. However, he couldn't do it if it entailed doing something that raised the visibility of his efforts and cost the company money and if the hypothetical chairman was unsympathetic.

"What I am saying is: A person of integrity -- below the chairman who was not so inclined to be compassionate -- could act with compassion -- could work things out within his department as long as it didn't rise to the level of visibility that would be noticed by the chairman.

"Putting aside the hypothetical -- at our Corporation there has been a commitment from the top down to accommodate disabled employees, and people of integrity are entrusted with power."

STUDY QUESTIONS

1. Compare "Corporate Compassion" with the "Compassionate Hospital". How did these organizations deal with situations where employees had disabilities arising out of long term illness?

2. What were the benefits and costs of the approaches taken by the business corporation and the hospital?

3. What would have been the fair and just thing for the organizations to have done? Why?

3. Both organizations were committed to compassion as a value. What does this require them to do in the stories? Does this require them to go beyond what is fair and just? Did they take any actions that went beyond what is just?

4. What would you have done?

5. The storyteller in the Compassionate Corporation said that the organization's integrity and compassion depended on the person with the ultimate power, the president or chairman. Do you agree or disagree? Why?

6. He felt the managers below the chairman could be compassionate only within their own units and so long as it was not noticed by the chairman if he was not similarly inclined. Do you agree or disagree and why?

YOU'RE FIRED

"Jack worked for me, and he was the controller of a large division of our company. We had just acquired this division that was in the business of manufacturing textiles, basically ski underwear and turtlenecks. The company had been owned by two business men who were prestigious and well known in their locality, but it was in a different part of the country than our headquarters. The two previous owners continued to run the business for us. Also, one of the owners -- he had been the president of the company-- became a member of our board of directors.

"About six months after we bought the company, the person resigned who had been controller for the previous owners. He didn't like the pressure of being part of a big publicly held company and its exact standards of reporting as well as all the tough audits he had to go through. So we hired Jack -- a young man with four or five years of experience after college. He happened to be a Notre Dame grad who went in there as the controller. He worked for the president [one of the two previous owners] of the division, but had a dotted line responsibility to the corporate staff that I headed up.

"As I said, the previous owners continued to run the division for us. One became the divisional president and the other became the divisional sales manager. Now they had another business, that they still owned, in Illinois. When we bought the division, they had said that the Illinois business was not related to the division we bought. The business, we bought, sold sportswear apparel -- none with pockets. They claimed that the equipment of our newly acquired division was not capable of making a shirt with a pocket. That was a lot of hot air-- I found out later -- but that is the story.

"This other business of theirs bought material from our newly acquired division. We shipped to their Illinois plant, and they finished the apparel and were supposed to ship the finished product back. We would sell the apparel to independent business men.

"So we kept shipping material to Illinois every week, and our new controller at the plant became suspicious because everything was being shipped out and nothing was being shipped back. He alerted me to that fact. He thought something was wrong -- was asking some questions. He was doing what he should be doing.

"Well, Jack went to lunch one day -- and when he came back-- he found an envelope on his desk from the divisional president. Remember, the divisional president was his boss and one of the two former owners.

"The note in the envelope told the young man that he was fired. He called me, and I talked with him. He told me that he had been with the divisional president that morning and was continuing his ongoing investigation. I said that the divisional president really didn't have the authority to fire him.

"We called the divisional president and asked him to come to our headquarters. At our meeting, that afternoon, he claimed the material was all there [at the divisional plant]. I told him that I had a plane ticket and was leaving the next morning. I told him that I would arrive at 8:00 AM to count the material in his plant. I said, 'You are welcome to come with me.' He declined. I had talked with my boss, the company president. We planned our strategy to deal with the situation. He was aware of the steps that I would take.

"I flew out there with another fellow from headquarters. It took us five minutes to count the material because there was no material there. We had been shipping material from our newly acquired division to the Illinois plant that the division president and his business partner still owned. Their Illinois plant was making shirts with pockets and shipping them to distributors, and never bothering to account to us for the material. He was cheating the company. He was putting the money in his pocket.

"We figured that they got about a quarter of a million dollars at that point. What happened was that one of the ex-owners -- the divisional sales manager-- made immediate restitution to the company. He was wealthy. He was a 'flighty' type of guy. He claimed that he was at the Illinois plant only once. The best we knew [was that] he was never out there much. He was just an investor with his buddy. We really don't know if he knew what was going on.

"This ex-owner [divisional sales manager] sued the other ex-owner [divisional president]. I testified in the case. The guy [divisional sales manager] won and got a judgment against him [the divisional president] but he had no assets. I don't think that the sales manager ever got anything out of his ex partner. By the way, the divisional sales manager kept his job.

"Jack -- the young man who was the divisional controller and the first to alert us of the problem -- was dismissed and given a very generous severance. We gave him the highest recommendation and helped him find another job. I don't think that he was out anything financially, but we couldn't keep him. I'm not too happy about that; but, under the circumstances, that's probably what had to happen. Here's a guy who did the right thing; saved the company some money; but, unfortunately, it cost him his job. He was a young guy, I'm sure that he had no problem. There were plenty of jobs. But it's something you don't want to do.

"We had a problem with the divisional president. Remember -- he was a member of our board. He was a stockholder since we purchased his company with stock. He was eventually terminated but it took a couple of months. We also got him to resign as a director, but it took awhile. It would have been impossible to keep Jack working there while the divisional president was still around.

"As I said, the ex-divisional president's partner sued him; and I testified in the case. I was a key witness. It was a sad situation. The ex-divisional president lost his community standing and eventually was a broken man. I remember being in the courthouse, and his wife coming up and nailing me. She said that I ruined her family, and her children were having nervous breakdowns. It was just a bad situation."

I asked the storyteller what he learned from this. He said, "When you find a situation like this, you just have to go and get it resolved. The point is that a guy -- like Jack -- does the right thing, but he is going to have to suffer because of the circumstances. As the controller, he did the right thing. I think that we were very generous with him money-wise; but, again, he had to go out and find another job. Sometimes, you are going to suffer a little bit when you do the right thing. But what are the alternatives? Just look the other way? That would have been worse. It would have gone on and on and on. He would have been implicated in it."

STUDY QUESTIONS

1. Do you agree with the storyteller that you have to suffer when you do the right thing? Disagree? Why?

2. What were the alternatives for Jack? What would you have done in his place? Why?

3. What were the alternatives for the storyteller? What would you have done in his place? Why?

4. How do you balance Jack's adherence to his professional code with his personal and financial security?

5 Can you expect that a manager to maintain his integrity when his actions harm his boss?

6. What parties were harmed in the story? Would it have been possible to work out a solution so that none of the parties would have been harmed? Or must the storyteller expect that some harm will be done no matter what action he takes?

7. What role does compassion play when a manager sees that his actions will harm some of the affected parties? How did the storyteller deal with this? How would you have dealt with it?

NO GUARDIAN ANGEL

"For the past two years, I was working in another city as a consultant with a national accounting firm, and I wasn't very happy in the job. I called the Vice President of Finance where I had worked before. He had been my boss; and, at that time, he was the controller. Since then, he was promoted to CFO. He said that there was an opening and that he would tell the new controller of my interest. The Controller called me and said that they had a position open in Planning -- that represented a promotion over what I was doing when I left the company. The Controller asked me to send a resume; and, later, I went for an interview. I also knew him when I had worked for the company.

"After I interviewed for the job, I heard, second hand, that opinion was divided on whether to hire me. The Controller wanted to hire me, but the CFO and some other people were against it. I think that the CFO opposed my coming back to the company -- even though I was a good employee -- because they felt I was disloyal for leaving.

"The CFO is a person who appreciates people who are loyal. He felt, I think, that I was unhappy with him and wasn't showing very much loyalty to him and the department that he was supervising at the time. He said nothing negative when I quit, but he did ask the reason why I was leaving. I told him that I wanted to finish my MBA studies. That was true; and I was thinking that maybe I might try another job -- some other type of work.

"My interpretation is that the CFO's emphasis on loyalty comes from his military background. He went to the navel academy and spent five years as a nuclear engineer on a submarine. From his background, he values somebody that is a team player. Somebody who is loyal to the team. At that point, it was his team -- it still is his team. The ironic thing is that he's not always real loyal to his staff. He's not afraid to let people go if he thinks it's necessary.

"I heard by 'scuttlebutt' that the new Controller presented a pretty strong case to hire me back. Evidently, he had to battle to hire me back. He felt that I had the skills necessary to do the work that he wanted done. Another person also came to my rescue and said kind things about me to get me re-hired.

"I was re-hired!"

I asked the storyteller whether the disagreements over re-hiring him had any negative consequences since he returned to the company. He said, "I see the CFO almost every day. He has his office just down the hall from my desk. He acts very cordial.

"The CFO values the Controller's opinion very highly. I think that they do things together outside the office. Their children play together. They golf together. The CFO respects the Controller's opinion."

I asked whether the Controller is loyal to the CFO. The storyteller said, "He is very loyal. He will do what he can to please the CFO, and the CFO will do what he can to make the Controller's life better too. The CFO said that he will help the Controller find something else within the company if the Controller isn't happy with what he doing. "

I asked the storyteller what he learned from this. He said, "I learned one thing about business. At least in the CFO's case, people who seem to get promoted are those who exhibit loyalty to him. They are people who are confident and don't make waves. Perhaps, rather, they pick and choose where they're going to make waves. They also support their decisions with valid arguments. I know a lot of people who are probably as intelligent as the Controller, but they have more abrasive personalities. So they are not recognized for their talents. The Controller is not the most talented person in the world, but it seems that he supports his stand with facts, logical thoughts, and reasoning. I think that type of individual will be promotable in the CFO's eyes, and he will be taken care of."

Have you come to the conclusion that it pays to be loyal, I said. "No. I think the CFO values loyalty. Many people value loyalty. When 'push comes to shove' -- when decisions are made to lay off people -- the cruel thing about business seems to be that relationships don't matter. Somebody either has the skills or doesn't have the skills, or the position and the people are not needed any more. Loyalty doesn't help anybody. You really still have to look out for yourself."

I asked, "Didn't the controller look out for you?" He said, "I think to some extent, the Controller looked out for me, but I also provided something that he needed. He wanted someone who could understand computer systems; someone who had some knowledge of computer jargon; someone who could analyze data and come to conclusions. He was having trouble finding that within the company. Having worked for the company, I had knowledge of its operation; and, working outside the company, I developed other skills that the Controller saw as valuable. I don't know whether he or anyone else in the company would give me a helping hand. More depends on whether I've got the skills they need."

STUDY QUESTIONS

1. Was ability a factor in their getting help? Or was it loyalty?

2. The storyteller in "A Helping Hand" saw his boss as a mentor, looking out for his development. The storyteller in "No Guardian Angel" saw his boss as looking out for his own needs when he fought to get the storyteller hired. What is your size-up?

3. Did compassion play a role in these stories? Explain.

4. Compare this story to "A Helping Hand". Did the storytellers in both stories get helped? What help did they get? Who helped them?

A LITTLE BIT DISAPPOINTED

A former student told me, "Jack and I managed similar activities except for different product lines. Well, the company reorganized; and the senior vice president gave a large chunk to Jack, and I was left without much." I asked, "Were you in line for the position?" He said, "Yes."

The former student said, "It bothered a lot of people that Jack was being brought along so quickly. Their evaluation was that he was very capable but had little experience even for the job he had before the reorganization. He also happened to be the senior vice president's son-in-law. Our peers were quite upset because they saw it as a signal that they would never get a promotion unless they were somewhat connected to some senior management people. From their point of view, it should be performance alone that should be used as the criterion for promotions rather than any type of personal relationships."

I asked him, "So your performance indicated that you merited the promotion. Is that right?" He said, "I think so, and I think other people in the organization did too. I don't mean to imply that a lot of people were upset that I wasn't given the position. I think it upset them from the sense that the wrong criterion was being used for promotion -- personal relationships rather than performance."

I asked, "So how did you react?" He said, "I was 'loaned out' to another part of the business, and the senior vice president said that he would look for another position for me in his division. In the meantime, they gave me something to do that I was interested in doing. They took good care of me."

I asked again, "How did you react." He said, "The senior vice president brought me into his counsel and explained his perspective in detail. And I could understand his point of view. His view, you may imagine, is totally different. Here is where he comes from: he travels a lot; he makes a lot of critical decisions; and he depends on people under him because he it not around to follow up. He needs people he can trust; that he knows well; he knows their response; that they are not going to do anything to ever undermine him. So he sees things like family relationships as building trust. Trust is built on relationships: people for whom he's done favors; people that have done favors for him; people that owe him favors. He feels they should be rewarded with upper level positions because of this issue of trust. From his viewpoint, he was doing what was best for the company."

I asked, "From your viewpoint?" My former student said, "He had no choice. He had to do what was best for the company."

I said, "He seemed to trust you enough to take you into his counsel and explain what he was doing. He seemed to have been straight forward with you. Was there some lack of trust?"

He said, "I don't think it was a lack of trust. I think it was an issue of did he have greater trust in Jack, his son-in-law. He spent more time personally with him as a family member and things like that."

I asked, "Do you think that he could have depended on you?"

He said, "Yes, uh-huh."

I asked, "How did you feel?"

He responded, "I was a little bit disappointed."

STUDY QUESTIONS

1. Did the senior vice president seem to show compassion for the former student? How? Did he show trust? Did he show fairness?

2. Do you agree with the senior vice president's view on trust? What would be your view in this situation?

3. How would you have handled the situation if you were the senior vice president? If you were the former student?

4. How were compassion, trust and fairness balanced in the story?

5. Compare the story to "A Helping Hand", "You're Fired", and "No Guardian Angel". Was compassion a factor in these stories? If so, how did it play out? How was compassion balanced with other considerations?

COLD HEARTED

The CEO of a fast growing business said, "I don't think there is as much point blank dishonesty as the world thinks. I'm a great admirer of most businessmen. I haven't known that many dishonest ones. I've know a lot of cold ones but not dishonest ones."

I asked him what he meant by cold.

The CEO said, "I struggle to fire people. I do it, but I die a thousand deaths every time. To take a person's job and say we don't need you any longer. We have a salesman who has been an under performer for some time, but he's a recovering alcoholic ever since I've known him. We are about ready to pull the strings. He started drinking again. I said he isn't going out of here until he's been given every chance in the world to solve his problems. Get him healthy, then we'll fire him. But I don't want to ruin a person's life -- I really don't. I pay money for that, and that is probably not fair to my shareholders, but I do it anyway."

I asked, "By carrying him?"

The CEO said, "Yes, I'll carry him until we can try to get him cured. We won't carry him forever. I know the guy pretty well. He can't find a job. He couldn't find a job even if he were sober. It would be difficult for him. He is not without talent. If we can get him cleaned up and his attitude straightened out, we could provide him a very good livelihood for the rest of his life -- if he wants to stay. Until we go through the process of making all that very clear to him, I won't toss him out."

The CEO said, "I fire people every week."

And I said, "Literally?"

He said, "No, I don't have to do it every week, but I give the nod. We've got 1,100 people. I force myself to do some of firings just because I never want it to get very easy. There is only three people reporting to me on the organization chart; but if one of the people on the next level is going to get fired, I usually do it myself because I never want it to get too easy.

"It is easier to fire someone if you don't have to look him or her in the eye. It is easier to sit here and say, 'That guy down there, he's out of here. Don't show me his face when he cries. Even shop floor employees. So it makes life easier if you can build a thick organization and insulate yourself from the people you're hurting. I won't do that."

STUDY QUESTIONS

1. The CEO said that he handles some of the firings so that it doesn't get too easy. What does he mean? What do you think of his decision to handle some of the firings? Why should he assume this task and not leave it to others

2. Cold executives, as meant by the storyteller, do not have compassion. They do not know the suffering that another has. Why then would cold executives wish to insulate themselves from the act of terminating another's employment?

3. Is compassion a virtue useful for managers of is it a hindrance?

PART VIII

AFTER-THOUGHTS

The stories are about events and people who sought to do what was right. The storytellers reflected on exemplary conduct that they had seen, and their stories suggest principles or virtues -- including: adherence to the law; avoiding harm; honesty; respecting others; justice in relations with stakeholders; keeping promises/commitments; and compassion. Each story highlights one of these virtues, but the stories also portray other virtues. The stories are unique with their interplay of virtues in different situations, yet several themes appear in many of the stories:

1. **Balancing virtues** to take the right action is a theme that occurred in many of the stories. The protagonists in the stories generally had to apply more than one virtue in their action so this led to balancing one virtue with another.

2. A second theme is the **reach of virtue** in the stories. Virtue was not action that was narrowly defined and self contained; but virtue in the stories was about the human condition, personal growth and leadership.

3. Virtue in the stories is a **view from the inside** -- inside the organization and introspective of the manager. It is not something that is seen on the outside of the organization -- by customers and other external stakeholders.

4. Virtue is an **ethical journey** for the storytellers. Something that was part of their everyday lives; a passage for the storytellers.

5. Exemplary conduct is **in the viewing** by the beholder. It comes from the heart so what some saw as virtue, others saw as wrong behavior. This does not imply relativism, but individual conscience.

6. Virtue is not a sure path but a **slippery slope** where the manager is not necessarily climbing upward but may be traversing along the side of the slope. The passage is slippery, and the footing is unsure.

7. Most of the storytellers believed that **virtue is rewarded**. They saw it as good business and related to their success, but a few felt that virtue was not rewarded. Instead, wrong conduct was good business.

1. BALANCING VIRTUES

A particular virtue was usually prominent in a story's action, but others were also at play and being balanced with each other. Balancing occurred in several ways. It could involve one virtue reinforcing a second; involve a virtue being applied at the expense of another; or involve friction between virtuous managers and their associates and competitors.

In some cases, the virtues were reinforcing each other. The story, "Integrity in Business", is about a senior executive who sought to compensate a vendor for up-front work by providing opportunities for future work. The storyteller was focusing on this executive's integrity but the action is played out in an atmosphere of trust created by open communication, honesty and promise keeping.

"Never Lie" is about an incident that illustrates the storyteller's belief that it is wrong to practice deception in business relations. Honesty is the prominent virtue in the story and it is complemented by the storyteller's (and his boss) strong sense of fairness and justice.

In some of the stories, virtues are practiced at the expense of each other. The emphasis is on adherence to the law in the story, "Returning a Gift", and the application of this principle limited the exercise of compassion. The protagonist returned a small gift given to him at a baby shower in his honor. The giver -- a friend but also a supplier to the protagonist's company -- felt that his action was misconstrued; but the protagonist felt that he could not "bend" his interpretation of the company's policy to accommodate his friend's feelings.

The protagonist in "Principled Action" was only beginning his career when he was faced with the dilemma of restoring property of a competitor that his firm had accidentally taken; or, on the other hand, keeping the material as ordered by the general manager. He saw restoring the property as the honest action to take while keeping the property as adherence to the company's code; and the code, he said, could be rationalized as fair. For him, integrity was to act honestly at the expense of adherence. He could not counter the directive of the general manager because of his subordinate position, but he resolved to leave the firm at the first opportunity. A short time later, he was fired after reporting to members of the Board that the general manager planned to take control of the firm. The protagonist's grandson said that his grandfather believed that individual freedom implied personal responsibility to do what was right. The dilemma between personal responsibility and adherence the company's code is difficult for someone at any stage of their career, but is especially difficult for a young person.

The balance struck among virtues can be offensive to people associating with the protagonist. A friendship cooled in the story, "Returning a Gift". In "Graying the Truth", a friendship was strained between the storyteller and his mentor. The storyteller first followed the course of action of his mentor and then rejected it as inconsistent with his values. The protagonist in "A Servant Leader: A Steadfast Tin Soldier" kept his promise to remain in the background and enable the sisters to retain their leadership of the college. This very commitment, however, led him to be self-effacing, and this posture led some to fear him and others to belittle him.

2. REACH OF VIRTUES

The stories are not about ethics in the narrow sense of a code of conduct or a theory for justifying actions, but it is about the human condition. The protagonists discover virtue in personal growth and leadership. For example, "The Servant Leader: A Steadfast Tin Soldier" portrays a style of leadership during a transformation of a college's direction, yet it is more than a style. The leader follows his heart -- from the bedrock of conviction of what is right. The story describes details of a very human situation where the anxieties of the participants interact with the leader's efforts to bring the college into strategic fit with its environment.

The story raises many questions. Was the self-effacing leader a product of the organization's particular vision; or does the story have wider application to American management? Executives often present themselves in a lordly manner with prominent trappings of prestige and power. Does the modest, unassuming leader provide an ethical alternative -- a leader who opens doors for others instead of having doors opened for him? Leaders who see themselves as servants.

The story, "Executive Parking"" suggests the same theme. Here the leader's servantship is symbolized by his forsaking an almost trivial trapping of status. The protagonists of "Rebuilding Business on Honesty" and "Breaking New Ground" both are leaders who acted as servants to their organizations.

Another example of virtue's reach is "Graying the Truth", where the storyteller grew in courage to apply his principles in the conduct of his business. His first response to a difficult situation was to imitate his mentor, but that was stressful for the storyteller because his action did not square with what he believed. After an internal struggle, he integrated his beliefs with his conduct and became his own person. Each of the stories touches the human condition, leadership and personal growth in some way.

3. VIEW FROM INSIDE

The storytellers' perspectives are from inside of their organizations. The stories are mostly about employees, owners and directors; and not about customers, investors and other stakeholders. Consequently, the stories are about "doing" since that is what insiders "see". Customers and other external stakeholders have less opportunity to "see" the conduct of the people in the organization. Instead, their emphasis is on the reputation of the business, its products and services. When I sought stories of leaders from external stakeholders, I found that they were usually unable to give instances of exemplary conduct but; instead, they told me about leaders' reputations. It seems virtue is the view from inside; and image, the view from outside.

4. ETHICAL JOURNEYS

The stories are not presented as blueprints for exemplary conduct, but they are peoples' ethical journeys -- how particular people applied their principles to situations and set out on what they saw as the right course of action. Their journeys are processes of growth in integrity with all the ups and downs that are experienced in acquiring integrity; and the journeys are a struggle to call things by their right names, to see things as they are, and distinguish reasons from rationalizations. Sometimes it seems that exemplary conduct ushers insight into what is virtuous. One does good things before understanding what is good.

The journey for one storyteller was how he, his project team and the company president made a promise and kept it even though it was not in their immediate interest to do so. This storyteller related in "His Word Was Good" that they did not disclose certain information to their company's data ser-

vice subsidiary even though the disclosure would have benefited that subsidiary and, therefore, the whole company. The
user subsidiaries had formed a project team to reengineer their
data systems, and the team wanted information from the competitors of the company's data services subsidiary. Up to that
time, they had applied software from the data services subsidiary. The competitors were hesitant about providing this information until the president promised that they would not disclose this information to the data services subsidiary, and they
did not. This stance made it possible for the storyteller and his
task force to design a system using software from several
sources. The president's keeping his word was admired by the
story teller and confirmed him in his own business journey.
They discovered the virtue of promise keeping by keeping
their promise.

In "A Helping Hand", the storyteller attributed his professional development to the guidance of his superior, and this
has led him to act in a similar manner in his own ethical journey. In "Accepting Responsibility When Things Go Wrong".
the storyteller concluded that it is better to stand up and accept
what happened, and that confirmed her stance in her work life.

Ethical decisions are sometimes only the beginning for
they can leave nagging and hard to resolve doubts about what
was really right. For example, the storyteller in the
"Compassionate Hospitals" struggled with whether they really
were working towards a compassionate culture or simply
preparing the hospitals for sale. Doubts seem to be part of the
journey because we are conducting ourselves in a highly complex and competitive environment. Virtuous executives are
constrained by market forces, interactions among stakeholders
and limited information. They might want but can not have the
intellectual and emotional certainty of Euclidean geometry, let
alone divine revelation. The executive can listen to his heart
and the immanent God, but they can expect a whisper at most,
not a sermon. Doubt is part of the journey.

Ethical journeys are a lifetime, and several stories relate a
lifetime of exemplary conduct. One executive is described in
three stories: "The Glass Ceiling"; "Obligations to Clients";
and "Standing for Autonomy". A second executive is de-

scribed in two stories: "Honesty as an Executive Style"; and "ESOP". These stories are about leaders who set an ethical climate in their organizations. The people who were interviewed respected them for their constancy and integrity. They lived business virtues of being tough-minded, courageous, compassionate and generous, and these are reflected during the course of their long business careers.

We contacted many executives who could not think of stories about exemplary conduct as noted in the introduction of the book. They said that they were not aware of such episodes. This was puzzling to me, and it is open to various interpretations (see the Introduction). One possible explanation relates to virtue as a journey. In their journeys, sometime or other, the storytellers reflected thoughtfully on the meaning of virtue in their actions. They may have come to understand virtue by contrasting virtuous and wrongful behavior. Again, they may have assembled the concept of virtue from personal values and experience. After a long time, they reached an understanding of the role of virtue in business and see virtue in themselves and others. Others have no stories to tell, perhaps, because they have not reflected on virtue in their journeys and are unable, therefore, to see exemplary conduct in themselves and others. The inability to relate exemplary conduct does not imply, however, that it does not exist -- only that it is not seen. The lack of reflection is understandable since management, in my view, is a profession that does not encourage reflection.

5. EXEMPLARY IS IN THE VIEWING

What one person sees as exemplary may not seem that way to others. Virtue is based on insight and discernment on the right thing to do so we can not be assured that our actions will be seen as virtuous. Theory can be used to rationalize and justify the action; but, in the end, it is a matter of judgment.

The story, "Executive Parking", is about an incident where a senior executive gave up his designated parking space, and this action was interpreted by the storyteller as a sign of the executive's respect for others. On the other hand, a reader saw the action as vacuous and pretentious. The reader's attitude was "Who cares whether the executive had to hike from his car to the building; and, anyway, he wouldn't be recognized by many employees."

In another instance -- "Accepting Responsibility When Things Go Wrong" -- the storyteller felt that the incident showed that company was willing to stand up and accept ownership for what happened and that employees were to do the same with regard to their mistakes. In contrast, a reader felt that the actions were motivated by public relations and were not a sincere effort to align the organization's conduct with its values.

In "Serving the Customer", the owner liquidated his business rather than sell a product that he felt did not fit the best interests of the user. The user was different from the buyer with the user often being a hospital and the buyer being a subcontractor. The subcontractor wanted lower prices and would accept wider specifications. The owner felt that the relaxed specifications were not appropriate for the expected use of the product. So the owner liquidated his business rather than "give the market what it wanted".

The owner's son reflected on the story and concluded that ethics is very expensive. He raised the question of what his Dad's decision might have been if he had not been able to afford what he did. The son concluded that his father had an iron will and was not going to backpedal, but the son wondered whether his dad made the right decision.

A reader felt that the owner's conduct did not make sense. The reader said that honesty required that he be straight forward about the product's capability, but the decision to buy the product was the buyer's responsibility. The reader operated in the same market structures and appreciated the issues facing the owner. The reader believed he had an obligation to make the specifications clear to customers, but customers' had the final say on the adequacy of the specifications. He felt that the right thing to do was to give customers what they wanted. The reader's view was that the "customer is king", and the virtuous act is to give customers what they want, not what he thought they should have. Is the reader's practice of virtue closer to the American vision than the owner's vision? I think so.

There are other examples where readers did not agree with whether the conduct was the right way. Virtue does not always make sense to the observer. Virtue is based on personal judgment so it does not assure uniform conduct within a culture and less so between cultures. The diversity of its practice presents a continuing challenge and fosters the quest for the right way.

6. SLIPPERY SLOPE

The stories illustrate that practicing virtue is like walking on a slippery slope. One does not have assured footing in picking the right course and remaining on course. In "Sticking to Our Promise", the storyteller hesitated about continuing the company's one bid policy when one of the bidders offered to change his bid, cutting the price substantially. The bidder took the position that reopening the bidding process would not violate the company's policy of permitting only one bid. The storyteller was inclined to reopen bidding because it would save money for the company, but his subordinate manager convinced him not to do this because his action would have broken the company's promise to vendors that only one bid would be permitted. Staying on course is not assured but the possibility of slipping is there.

The protagonist in "Graying the Truth" struggled with what course of action to follow; he set out on a course but came to regret this course. He had a change of heart on how to live his business life and integrated his beliefs with his conduct.

The storyteller and his organization struggled to create a compassionate culture in "Compassionate Hospitals". The organization has difficulty in discerning what constituted compassion in its setting. On the one hand, the managers and staff were compassionate in helping employees, patient and their families who were having personal difficulties; but, on the other hand, the organization was insensitive to harassment issues.

The hospital strove to keep its footing on the slippery slope but did not. The storyteller was committed to creating a compassionate culture and worked diligently to make this happen in his own life and the life of the organization. Then something happened that brought down the compassionate culture and harmed the storyteller. The hospital slipped down its slope, but its value on the market probably increased. The storyteller continues his ethical journey outside the organization.

7. IS VIRTUE REWARDED?

Most storytellers and readers believed that exemplary conduct was good business, and they were confident in that view. A few were not convinced that virtue is good business. This gives rise to a puzzling question: do executives use this belief to explain why they act in an exemplary way? In other words, does exemplary conduct need to be justified as good business to be accepted in a free market economy?

On the other hand, have they 'counted' the business payoff from virtue that shows them that it is good business? Have storytellers found from their experience that exemplary conduct has paid off?

The storyteller of "Integrity in Business" believed that exemplary conduct was good business. He said, "It is really amazing how a single transaction had so much significance for us and would not have happened except for the Vice Chairman's integrity." Open communication, honesty and keeping one's promises built a relationship of trust and integrity between personnel in the two companies; and this relationship enabled one of the organizations to build a new business and the other to receive reliable service in a market where outcomes were ambiguous.

In "Never Lie", some business was lost in the short run because the protagonist would not give one customer an advantage over other customers, but the business was not hurt in the long run. The reason was not related to his not lying, he thought, but to the decline in the importance of that segment of the business. None the less, the storyteller was affirmed in their policy of never lying by this incident.

The storyteller in "Graying the Truth" found that his business has been successful since he has been up-front with his clients. The company had been less than open with a client to save business, but this experience set them on a course of honesty.

The storyteller, in "Putting It Back Together", believed that respect led to creating a cooperative team. He said that the new executive director treated people with respect and did not allow staff to blame each other in their contentious and fractured organization. He was able to turn the organization around without any blood letting and was able to build a cooperative team. It was the same people with a new spirit that became a successful and productive team.

In "Sticking to Our Promise", The storyteller did not alter the company's bidding process although it stood to gain by receiving a lower bid. The long term consequences have been good business, he found. The vendors are now more attentive to the company's interests, and the company is getting better service.

Some of the storytellers doubted that virtue was good business. In the "Open Drawer", the storyteller noted that the salesman who bribed the purchasing manager was prosperous while the one who did not was "shabby".

The storyteller in "People Felt Manipulated" admired the virtue of the new superintendent but he yearned for the unambiguous environment of the former superintendent who manipulated the staff. The new superintendent was open in his communication with the staff about his thinking and the contingencies facing the organization. This created uncertainty about the future in the mind of the storyteller. The former superintendent withheld information and gave different information to various staff to create a more controlled environment. The storyteller believed that he was able to contribute more in the context of the more open situation; but he saw the old situation as more efficient.

Some saw virtue as its own reward. They saw satisfaction in doing the right thing. In "Professional Honesty", the story-teller felt that his former firm could have finessed the opportunity, and he would have never known that he lost this opportunity. His former associates gained nothing by passing the information to him. They did it, he felt, to adhere to their code of professional conduct.

The senior executive in "Executive Parking" got some praise and, perhaps loyalty, by giving up his privileged parking, but he got a reaction of indifference from other senior executives in the company. The skepticism of readers suggest the possibility that the same occurred within the organization. The payoff from his action seems problematic. He would seem to have committed himself to giving up executive privilege because he believed that it was the right way to act.

In "Treating People Fairly", the president's act of generosity gave him no business advantage. He persuaded the Board to set aside some of the gain from the bank's sale for employees who themselves would not gain. They had not been able to purchase the bank's shares for one reason or another, and many would be terminated as their functions were consolidated into the acquiring bank. They had contributed to the bank's growth and its attractiveness as an acquisition candidate so the president felt that they should benefit from the acquisition. Their gain came from the bonus that the Board had decided to award to the president.

The president received the employees' admiration for being fair when it brought him no gain. Their loyalty was not translated into productivity or other material gains and brought down to the "bottom line" since the president was leaving -- and many of these employees would be leaving. Admiration can be seen as a reward for virtue, but its link to "good business" is tenuous in this episode. The storyteller conveyed the impression that the president had been constant in being fair over his business career, and this suggests that virtue was his reward.

The protagonist in "Downsizing" worked out early retirement packages so employees could leave the firm with "their heads held high". He said that he would rather spend the additional money to enable employees to make the most of their later years. He did not suggest that there was any benefit for the firm in doing this, but said that it was the "right thing, the ethical thing". He probably could have been pressed to rationalize his action as improving morale and productivity, but he did not offer this justification.

Whether virtue is good business and/or is its own reward was resolved by the storytellers for their situations. This is not a question of statistical significance, but a matter of belief and experience. It is influenced by one's values and beliefs, business culture, and the values of others.

Machiavelli, it would seem, saw a sharp contrast between virtue and success. He advised the Prince that he would be well off to adapt his ways of doing things to the circumstances.[1] Executives, within this perspective, are more likely to fail when they are concerned with virtuous action rather than practical action. Yet the storytellers did not see this sharp contrast between virtue and success. For most of them, the practical and the ethical blend together. Some of the stories describe action that is good management practice so the ethical seemed to be the practical thing to do and be in the decision maker's best interest. The story about the Servant Leader was like this. His practice of virtue looked like good management because he was successful. It would not have looked like good management, however, if he had failed. Other stories describe situations where the ethical was not practical. "Serving the Customer" was a situation where the owner had the opportunity to be profitable. If he had been practical in his approach to the customer the storyteller felt that his father would have been successful. He would not do what was necessary to succeed, and he acted to liquidate the business because he could not serve the user the way he ought.

I believe that we need to admit both possibilities. The ethical accompanies business success, but it can also accompany failure. Integrity calls for living with both success and failure. The stories' exemplars followed their consciences, not

---

[1]Dunne, op. cit., pp. 164-165.

society's demands. It is a question of belief and judgment -- one's view of the world. I believe that virtue is its own reward, and the reward of good business is an extra bonus.

Besides business success, there is the question of whether virtue is rewarded with personal success -- career advancement and power. A person reading the stories asked me the question: Can persons of virtue be trusted with power? Can they rise in an organization where their boundaries for decisions are no longer set by superiors? The reader's belief was that they could not be trusted with power, and there was a 'virtue ceiling' that limited the advancement of people with integrity.

The storytellers were startled when I asked these questions. At first glance, the question seems like a contradiction. Trust and virtue would seem to go together. A virtuous person has integrity and can be trusted to do what is right. However, that is the rub. If they can be expected to do what is right, then can they trusted to do what their sponsors want? The response of the storytellers when I asked this question was, "that depends on the what the sponsor wants." The usual response was that some sponsors expected their protégés to do the right thing because that is what they would do. Others expected them to do what served the interests of the sponsor, and to bend their principles to make it happen. From the view of the storytellers, both situations happened; and the book contains many examples of both.

In "Pressure from Above", the storyteller was pressured to approve payment of inflated expenses as side payments that would not be recorded as part of the price of the business. The storyteller refused and later left the company. He had a successful career elsewhere after this incident, but he might have achieved fame and power if he had 'played ball' with his boss. Despite this experience, his attitude was that a virtuous executive could be trusted with power and that his experience was an exception.

In "The Compassionate Corporation", three successive CEO's (including the present one) exercised power with compassion toward disabled employees. From the viewpoint of the storyteller, they were virtuous men and were selected for leadership positions of a large multi-national corporation.

None of those interviewed took the position of the reader that people with integrity were not trusted with power, but many offered examples where they were not trusted. However the interviewees were mostly optimistic that power and integrity were joined together in business.

ASSESSING ONE'S INTEGRITY

Business executives can assess their constancy and integrity. The place to begin is to tell one's own story. It may be an ethical journey or a single incident; it may be something highly acclaimed or met with skepticism and offense; it may be a constant focus on one principle or matter of balancing principles; it may be conducted on a slippery slope or on high ground; or it may be seen as good business or accepted as its own reward.

One can reflect on episodes of exemplary conduct that are their own or on episodes of others that they have viewed closely. This reflection is very difficult because business is not accustomed to introspective thinking. A help is to make a list of all possible values and select those that have the highest priority for one. This book lists those that I have encountered in my interviews, but there are many more values that should be included on one's initial list. A comprehensive list of fifty values in contained in *Organizational Vision, Values and Mission*[1] The book also provides a simple but effective technique for ranking the values.

One can reflect on the virtues that one has given the highest priority. Consider incidents where these virtues have been applied. If there are no incidents then one might reconsider the

---

[1]Cynthia D. Scott, Denies T. Gaffe and Glenn R. Toe,
Organizational Vision, Values and Mission (Menlo Park, California: Crisp Publications, Inc., 1993).

priority of the value. Creating one's story of exemplary conduct provides a base on which to set one's direction.